Praise for WHERE DOGS GO TO LIVE!

"*Where Dogs Go to Live: Inspiring Stories of Hospice Dogs Living in the Moment reads like a Chicken Soup for the Soul®* book. The positive, up-lifting energy expressed throughout is a clear indication as to how these dogs transform to live life to the fullest in their twilight. The stories in this book will deeply touch your heart and remind you about the best of what it means to be fully human living your purpose."

–Jack Canfield, Coauthor of *Chicken Soup for the Dog Lover's Soul*

"The terrible misfortunes of homelessness and a terminal diagnosis usually result in despair and hopelessness. But not at Monkey's House. *Where Dogs Go to Live: Inspiring Stories of Hospice Dogs Living in the Moment* provides a glimpse into the joy, happiness, and innumerable life lessons learned by living with and loving dogs as they die. A few of these gems captured in this book can teach us all to be better at what dogs innately master: living joyfully in the moment. It is said that 'life is a series of moments remembered'; Monkey's House captures the few remaining moments of terminal dogs' lives and makes each day magical for them. The results are indelible memories of life, love, and connection for both the dogs and the people caring for them. This book is a collection of stories about those relationships."

–Karen Shaw Becker, Wellness Veterinarian

"*Where Dogs Go to Live* is a must-have book for every dog lover's shelf. It chronicles the extraordinary work of Monkey's House a Dog Hospice & Sanctuary in New Jersey that is, quite literally, heaven on earth for older dogs who have little time left. You'll find yourself falling in love with all the happy, contented dogs featured in the pages of this book, and you'll quickly see that a dog hospice is not a sad place to be. Instead, it is an oasis of compassion, kindness, meaning, and love."

–Laura T. Coffey, author of the national best seller, *My Old Dog: Rescued Pets with Remarkable Second Acts*

"I started reading this book during Covid-19 shelter in place; needless to say, it was the book I needed! Uplifting stories of dogs and people and of love, kindness, and second chances, reminding us all of the healing qualities that dogs and people have together and the compassion we carry with us. Thank you for putting pen to paper and sharing these journeys. Now let's hope everyone runs out and saves a senior dog!"

–Sherri Franklin, Founder and CEO Muttville
Senior Dog Rescue, CNN *Top10 Hero 2016*

"Michele and Jeff have created a 'family' that allows many lucky dogs and volunteers to discover: Dogs reflect their humans' love; Dignity and quality of life matter as much as how long we share that life; Frustration and heartbreak are inevitable, especially when facing abuse, neglect, the justice system for animals; The rewards are great.

Watching the joy of a dog's 'new life' blossoming before our eyes drives all involved in senior dog rescue and hospice. No old dog should die feeling abandoned. *Where Dogs Go to Live* expresses this very well and hopefully will inspire others."

–Judith and Lee Piper, Founders, Old Dog Haven

"*Where Dogs Go to Live*" is an inspiring tribute to senior dogs and the incredible work that Monkey's House does to help them live the remaining chapters of their lives to the fullest! A fabulous resource for anyone with a senior dog as well as a heartwarming read for anyone who loves animals!"

–Dr. M. Noelle Knight, VMD, PhD

"This beautiful and heartwarming book is exactly what we all need during difficult times. It gives me hope that the world is good in its essence and that experiencing loss may give us an opportunity to witness the deepest love. Thumbs up to you for writing on this important topic. A must read for every dog lover!"

–Dr. Peter Dobias, DVM, founder and CEO,
Dr. Dobias Healing Solutions, Inc.

WHERE DOGS GO TO LIVE!

Colleen,

There is nothing better than the love of an old dog.

Best Wishes,

Jeff Allen

WHERE DOGS GO TO LIVE!

Inspiring Stories of Hospice Dogs Living in the Moment

JEFF ALLEN
with Michele Allen
foreword by Larissa Wohl

Best Chapter Publishing LLC
Southampton, NJ

ISBN (paperback): 978-1-7351810-0-4
ISBN (ebook): 978-1-7351810-1-1

For more information, visit www.monkeyshouse.org

Cover and interior design by Christy Collins, Constellation Book Services

Printed in the United States of America

DEDICATION

This book is dedicated to all the hospice dogs that find themselves homeless at a point in their lives when they need their family the most. To the dogs that were lucky to call Monkey's House their home, but even more so to the ones that "disappeared" into the back of a shelter. I dedicate this book to you; your lives did matter. We are sorry you were let down in your time of need. In our hearts and souls, you are on this journey with us. You will never be forgotten.

LA and Mattie, finding peace and
friendship at Monkey's House.

CONTENTS

SENIOR DOGS ARE THE NEW PUPPIES!

BY LARISSA WOHL, PET RESCUE EXPERT

As a pet rescue expert, I see so many beautiful, loving, and heroic animals that will never know the love of a family…and that stands especially true for senior dogs. Senior dogs are often over-looked because of a myriad of reasons, and trust me, I've heard them all. They're no longer as cute or fluffy, have too many medical issues, won't be around for long, and so on. Hearing all these excuses time and time again absolutely breaks my heart because I know from MANY personal experiences that loving, and being loved by, a senior dog is a gift from above! They provide never-ending laughter, companionship, and comfort. They're also easy, relaxed, grateful, and provide a peace of mind you'll never get when adopting a young dog because "what you see is what you get." You already know their temperament, how they are with kids, how they are with dogs, their exercise needs, and so on. Hence, there are no surprises!

With that said, for reasons I'll never understand, not everyone shares my love of senior dogs! And that's exactly why I was so honored to work with Michele and Jeff Allen. Michele came to Los Angeles a couple of years ago to be a guest for a segment on Hallmark Channel's *Home & Family*. As the on-camera pet rescue expert, I'm always scour-ing the internet for heartwarming stories that truly capture the magic and unconditional love animals bring us and vice versa. As soon as I read about Monkey's House and their unwavering dedication to help the neediest animals, I knew their story had to be shared.

Whether or not you caught the segment about the inspirational sanctuary Michele and Jeff have created, "*Where Dogs Go To LIVE!*" is a must-read and dives even deeper into the power senior dogs possess and how rescuing one is like winning a first-class ticket on the "Your Outlook on Life Will Never Be the Same" train.

Whether it's the story of broken Bea and her beautiful transformation or three-year-old Kaiden, a young boy with special needs who finds safety and strength fostering senior dogs, you'll be reminded that animals have the power to make us better humans.

Where Dogs Go To LIVE! is an ode to rescuers and senior dogs everywhere. Thank you, Jeff and Michele, for giving senior dogs a voice and creating a beautiful family of rescuers, volunteers, and fans that are helping spread Monkey's House's impactful message.

Larissa Wohl is using her voice to help the voiceless. Through her on- and off-camera efforts, she's helped thousands of animals find their forever homes. Currently Larissa can be seen daily as the host of Hallmark Channel's Adoption Ever After *initiative for the network's morning show,* Home & Family. *As part of the initiative, Larissa showcases two adoptable animals a day and provides weekly segments to help pet parents with various issues such as pet safety, education about animal rescue, and how to enrich pet lives. She's also part of the Hallmark Channel's highly rated* American Rescue Dog Show.

Larissa with her three rescues, Muppet, Maple, and Piggly.
Photo courtesy of Ben Shani Productions

INTRODUCTION

Driving down our country road, you'll pass field upon field of blueberries, corn, and soybeans. We're nestled between the New Jersey Pine Barrens and prime farmland; there's even a small vineyard behind our property. This is when you might wonder if you are actually in New Jersey. Most people think of New Jersey as a dense urban setting, an extension of New York City. We are located in the southern portion of the state that still lives up to the state's tagline, the "Garden State." As you turn into the driveway, our home looks like any other Cape Cod house sitting on six acres with a small barn and some other buildings. From its ordinary outward appearance, you would never guess the true mission of Monkey's House nor realize the amount of love that resides inside that dwelling.

Heading down our lane, you might see a couple of bunnies playing in the front field. If you're lucky, you may even catch a glimpse of wild turkeys with their brood of chicks passing by. Exiting the car, watch where you step as a small flock of free-ranging chickens roam the property; they often leave their calling cards behind. Feeling the sun on your face, you glance up and notice the bright blue sky with a few cumulus clouds strategically placed, creating a beautiful backdrop for this special visit.

"It's so peaceful and quiet, where is all the barking?" you say to yourself.

Suspense builds as you're about to meet the dogs of Monkey's House. As you walk up the ramp toward the front door in anticipation, you hear a deep purring sound. Looking down, you find yourself welcomed by a typical tabby farm cat. Approaching you, his back begins to round ever so slightly upward as he gently leans into your leg, his way of saying, "Hello, my name is Grandpa, and I'm the cutest one here."

Kneeling down, you give Grandpa a few strokes and catch yourself wondering, "Am I at the right house?" You are; you've arrived at Monkey's House. Grandpa is just one of our personal rescues who thinks he's a dog; please don't disillusion him.

You're about to experience something unique and magical. Even seasoned dog trainers and rescue leaders are in awe of what they've seen and felt at Monkey's House. Entering the house, you are greeted by dogs of varying breeds, sizes, ages, and activity levels. You make your way quickly into the family room to take a seat as dogs gather from all directions. You may opt to settle into a comfortable chair or to plop yourself on the floor to be closer to the wet noses and wagging tails. After a minute or two, the dogs begin to calm down and let you know the petting can begin! The family room looks somewhat typical with the exception of about a dozen dog beds, sofas, and chairs from small to large sizes throughout. The pups make sure that wherever you choose to sit, it will be the best seat in the house.

There's a saying at Monkey's House, "An empty lap is a wasted lap." There will be pups at your feet waiting to hop aboard, and most likely you'll end up with Maisey, a little miniature pinscher, on your lap taking ownership of you during your visit. As you stroke her hair, something will seem out of the ordinary; there's a sense of serenity throughout the room. To be honest, at about this time of the gathering, all our visitors notice something a little amazing—twenty dogs all content, living together, sharing beds, and snuggling. There is no barking, but you do hear the occasional snoring; that's most likely one of our beagles, Lucy or Mr. Peebody.

Looking at the walls, you'll see photos of dogs everywhere, current residents and those that made their way to the Rainbow Bridge, a very special place in heaven reserved for all of our furry friends. You'll see individual and group photos alike, but what most attracts your attention are the pictures of the Monkey's House crew, dogs and volunteers with Santa, and field trips to places like the Jersey Shore and the local parks. The photos show our hospice dogs *living*, loving old friends and new acquaintances alike. A picture is worth a thousand words and dispels everything you've ever heard about old dogs.

You'll begin to wonder, "Is this really a hospice? These dogs look so happy and are really enjoying life." Like many who have visited before you, you might ask what gave us the inspiration to start Monkey's House. This is our story.

CHAPTER 1

SO IT BEGINS:
OPENING A NEW DOOR

Michele and I both grew up with pets as part of our families. Dogs, cats, horses, you name it; between the two of us, we've probably had it. As a young boy, I remember the dogs I grew up with like it was yesterday. Our family was partial to larger dogs. The first dog I remember was a boxer named Chita; followed by Odie, a large German shepherd; and finally Ginger, an Irish/English setter mix. Each dog had its own personality: Chita was playful; Odie was the protective one; and Ginger was loving and always ready to chase birds. Growing up, we didn't have video games or computers to keep ourselves entertained, so we made our own fun. We were usually outside roaming the woods with our trusted four-legged friend by our side. If the neighbor kids and I were riding our stingray bikes, our dogs weren't far behind running along-side us on the journey.

Michele grew up loving horses so much she'd spend every free moment with them and a dog by her side, preferably horseback riding if weather and time permitted. Michele grew up with a little black mutt named Tramp, as in *Lady and the Tramp*. Trampy, as she liked to call her, lived up to her name as she was very straggly and followed Michele everywhere.

Once married, we quickly got our first dog together, a shepherd-husky mix that we named Zavy. He came from a nearby shelter, our first rescue together. He was eight weeks old and the cutest puppy ever. (Of course, we think that about all our babies.) Shortly after Zavy came a pair of rescue cats, Larry and Darrell. Michele missed having a horse while she was in college and during the first few years of our marriage, so you can guess what came next—a horse named Bourbon. The suburbs are good for a dog and two cats, but throwing a horse into the family mix meant we needed to move to a house with more land and a small barn. That's exactly what we did. We found a house perfect for our expanding family. One horse grew into two. Horseback riding ended up being a nice pastime that we could share as a couple. On most weekends, you could catch us trail riding together in the Pine Barrens. Michele and I found solace with our family of four-legged children.

Through the years, we moved a couple more times for my job, eventually settling down very close to our first house just in the next town over. Our current home is that little farm I just described in Southern New Jersey. We've lived twenty years at our current residence, and throughout that time we've had horses, goats, chickens, geese, and ducks to go along with our dogs and cats. Michele and I both agree that this house is by far our favorite. The old saying, "Home is where the heart is," speaks volumes, and Monkey's House is full of heart.

Our rescue habits escalated at this house. Raising backyard chickens became the craze in the early 2010s, and we had some friends jump on the bandwagon. They were shocked early one morning when they heard "cock-a-doodle-doo." You guessed it; that was no chicken but a rooster waking up about fifty other families in their townhouse complex! They had two options: Since the one involving a pot was out of the question, they turned to us. The rooster was spared and came to the country to live out the remainder of his life with us. We had also been given ducks that outgrew their kiddie pools. Those ducks must have thought they hit the jackpot going from a plastic pool to a quarter-acre pond in our backyard! And so it was that many different animals found their way into our family with open arms.

Neighbors are far and few between where we live, a huge plus when you have as many different types of animals that we've had over the years. In the evenings, we would walk in the back field with our dogs on leashes followed closely by a pair of goats, two horses, a cat, and a goose named Hootie. (Hootie thought she was a horse—she ate grain out of my horse Brit's feed bucket and grazed with him in the field.) No doubt a passerby would have done a double take at that parade. At the time, we were doing "pack walks" and didn't even realize it.

If you've ever had dogs, you'll know that they seem to gravitate to "their person." Sure, they love everyone in their family, but some really attach themselves to one special person, and when you're the person they've chosen, there isn't a better feeling in the world. There's this feeling of unconditional love you only get from a dog, the "you can do no wrong" look in its eyes. A few years after we rescued Zavy, we had two other pups join the family, Bee Gee and Emmy. Once Zavy passed, the two remaining dogs chose their persons: I was Bee Gee's person and Michele was Emmy's. When Emmy passed, Michele felt a hole in her heart. Even though we still had Bee Gee, whom she loved, the emptiness wouldn't go away. One day, she called her friend Joanne who worked at a local shelter, the Voorhees Animal Orphanage. Michele explained the emptiness she was feeling and told Joanne she wanted to adopt a dog.

This was years before Monkey's House was founded, but I believe this may have been the tiny spark that put the slow burn into Michele and that eventually brought me on board. Emotionally, Michele couldn't bring herself to go into the shelter to see all the unwanted dogs, so she asked Joanne about the dogs available for adoption and to choose the one nobody else wanted. Joanne picked out Poncho, a little mixed breed with a severe heart condition. Michele met Joanne at the gate to pick up Poncho. While Michele and I had talked at length about getting another dog, and when she said Joanne found her one, I was excited to see him, but honestly, I wasn't sure I was ready to add one to our household. Well, to my surprise, when I got home from work that day, there was Poncho…and McKinsey!

First, you're probably laughing, and secondly, you're asking, who is this McKinsey character? She was a character for sure, a little thirteen-plus-year-old shih tzu that was dumped by her owners who wanted her euthanized because, as they put it, "She's just too old." As it turned out, McKinsey and I adored each other. She would meet me at the front door every evening; when she barked, her whole body levitated off the floor. I would reach down and pick up this little twelve-pound angel, and she would place one paw on my shoulder and cross her back legs as if she were sitting in a lounge chair as I carried her around the house to greet Michele. Thankfully, those "few months" that McKinsey was expected to live turned out to be over three and a half years!

Around this time, we started to foster dogs, not your average dogs but those with medical conditions other fosters didn't have the ability to care for. I'm not saying I would have been able to care for them either back in the early days, but Michele is another story. Michele has her RN BSN, was a nurse for many years, and she's very comfortable with medically challenged dogs. I have to say Michele is a special breed altogether. If you were in the hospital, you would want Michele as your nurse. She was a patient's advocate 100 percent, arguing with doctors when necessary to ensure her patients got what they needed. She was awarded Nurse of the Year in 1997 for her skills, compassion, and due diligence.

Michele half-jokingly says that her nursing career prepared her for Monkey's House. She shows that same dedication to the dogs; there is no cutting corners. The local rescues saw this quality in Michele and began reaching out to her with their difficult medical cases. One such case was a twelve-year-old golden retriever named Goldie. She was extremely thin and had a very large tumor on her abdomen. They asked us to foster Goldie, hoping Michele could get her to gain weight before she had surgery to remove the tumor. Michele tried everything but couldn't get Goldie to gain weight. She believed the tumor was cancer.

When you foster a dog for a shelter, you use the shelter veterinarian and go by his or her medical diagnosis. One major problem with that is that shelters are limited in funds for the many dogs they have in their care. Most shelter veterinarians try to do their best with what they have, but sadly at times that's just not good enough, especially for Michele. She took Goldie to another veterinarian for another opinion. We gladly paid for the examination ourselves. As Michele assumed, it was a very bad diagnosis. Goldie did have cancer. The surgery was cancelled; Goldie had only weeks to live.

Upon hearing the diagnosis, Michele turned to me and said, "We have to adopt Goldie." I was a little confused as we were already fostering her. (When you *foster*, you agree to take in a homeless dog and give it love, care, and attention, generally until the dog is *adopted*. In a sense, you're acting like a satellite location for the larger rescue organization.) Michele firmly stated, "Goldie is not going to heaven without an 'official' family." So, we adopted Goldie Allen and soon after assisted her to the Rainbow Bridge. Since Goldie, no dog that we have ever cared for left for the Rainbow Bridge without becoming an Allen first.

If adopting Poncho and McKinsey were the sparks, then Goldie was the kindling that started a movement in us, a movement that became a small fire.

MONKEY—THE LITTLE GUY THAT INSPIRED IT ALL!

By the time Monkey came into our family, we had grown to nine dogs split between our own personal pups and fosters. Monkey joined us on a brisk fall afternoon. Michele didn't tell me he was coming; she believes I always take the news about a new foster dog better if the dog is already in the house. To be honest, I may have been a little grumpy about the number of dogs we had back then and reluctant to bring another dog into the house. However, Michele had good persuasion skills. She would give me "the talk"; I would gripe for a few days, all the while falling in love with the dog. But there was something different about Monkey.

After a day at work, as I walked through the front door, I could see Michele was preparing to give me the talk, but I immediately noticed Monkey. He started spinning in circles as if to greet a long-lost friend.

In the blink of an eye Monkey was nestled in my arms. I'm not sure who was smiling more, Michele, Monkey, or me. No talk, no questions, no looks, just smiles.

Monkey came to us for end-of-life care. He had *congestive heart failure* (CHF), which made him constantly short of breath and turned his gums blue. Although he struggled to breathe, he was happy. As a foster dog, his medical needs were supposed to be handled by the shelter's veterinarian. Unfortunately, this veterinarian had no interest in doing anything to help Monkey get comfortable. Michele had asked him for scripts, offering to pay for Monkey's medication.

He refused, saying, "He's just a little shelter dog. He won't be around long, a week, maybe three at most. Just enjoy him while he's here." Michele said she will never forget those words, words that were burned into her soul and of course unacceptable to both of us.

We adopted Monkey so that we could get him the care he needed. We knew he was going to die, but that didn't mean we weren't responsible for his care. His respirations were often about eighty breaths a minute; a healthy dog's respirations are around twenty per minute. Any asthmatic can tell you what it's like being short of breath, struggling to get oxygen into the lungs. We had prior experience with dogs in CHF and knew there were many inexpensive medications that would make him more comfortable. So off we went to our veterinarian to get him the care and the prescriptions the shelter veterinarian wouldn't prescribe him.

Monkey started to improve. Next stop, the cardiologist. We never once kidded ourselves about his condition. We were realistic but still fought hard for his time with us. He stabilized and started to thrive. He greeted each and every day with a zest for living. He never missed an opportunity to make us smile, and we became more charmed and appreciative of his silly antics. Monkey loved dogs—big ones, little ones, crazy ones—and he especially loved us. But he bit or tried to bite everyone else. Lucky for us, we live in a remote area so he had little opportunity to bite anybody.

As Monkey improved, it became clear that his infected teeth caused him terrible, constant pain, so much so that at times he didn't want to eat, and his tiny muzzle was swollen. Our veterinarian at the time, Dr. Sarah Ball-Garino, said a dental procedure was the only way to improve his quality of life. And so, the prep for his dental work began. Monkey was on antibiotics for one week each month, and we checked in with the cardiologist who said that because of Monkey's condition, anesthesia put him at high risk. But the cardiologist also knew we didn't really have a choice.

Michele was extremely concerned about the procedure because of Monkey's CHF. The day of the procedure, Dr. Ball-Garino had kindly invited Michele to hang in the waiting room with Monkey rather than to just drop him off, which was customary. Dr. Ball-Garino came out herself to get him and had to wrap him up like a burrito as Monkey planned to eat her for lunch.

Monkey's dental operation didn't take that long, but to Michele it felt like hours. Michele had also taken along Sora, one of our other dogs, to keep Monkey company. Honestly, I think she took Sora to keep herself calm as they walked the neighborhood around Dr. Ball-Garino's office several times that morning. (You'll read about Sora's story in chapter 2, "Welcome to the Family.") All of the planning, coordinating, worrying, and praying paid off. Monkey came through the surgery just fine, losing all of his green, rotting teeth with the exception of his signature canines. (*Canines* are the long, pointed teeth found toward the front of a dog's mouth. These are often referred to as *fangs*.)

Monkey showing off his canines.

It's amazing the difference a healthy mouth makes in a dog's life, and Monkey was no exception. With a healthy mouth and just his canines, he was able to eat pain-free and take the proper heart medication. Monkey was truly enjoying his life, and we enjoyed every day with him. He especially liked his walks with his brothers and sisters around the back field. We had a few dogs that could be "off leash"; Monkey was what we called "dropped leash." He would have a leash on, but at times we would drop it so he could really play with his buddies. With his CHF, we had to keep a close watch to make sure he didn't overdo it. If it looked like he needed a rest, we would just grab his leash.

Monkey had a stride like a galloping horse. Both of his front legs would stretch as far out in front of him as possible, hit the ground, and propel him forward. He ran like a champion thoroughbred heading for the homestretch in the Kentucky Derby. We would give a shout-out, and he'd quickly turn and zoom back toward us, almost as if he were saying, "Look at me, look at me." As he zipped past, he would spin and with the biggest smile, jump up, place his front paws on my thigh, and look for a pat on the head.

Over time, Monkey's health began to wane, but he still came along on our walks. His dropped-leash time was limited, but he didn't seem disappointed as he had a new ride, literally, in my arms. If it looked like he had enough, I would pick him up, and he would enjoy the scenery at a different vantage point. We still made sure he had time to do his "zoomies"; we just supervised them.

Even as Monkey's health deteriorated, he was very adaptable. Although his walks were a little shorter and he had to limit his exertion, Monkey found something else to be excited about and that he undoubtedly found amazing. One day, when Michele took Monkey to the veterinary office with Sora along to keep him company, they stopped at the bank drive-thru. When the transaction was completed, the nice teller sent a couple of dog biscuits through the pipe for the pups. Monkey got so excited he instantly fell in love with the drive-thru. I'm sure that evening Monkey was telling all his brothers and sisters,

"There's this lady who sits behind a window and just hands out treats for dogs; it's GREAT!" Near the end of his life, Michele was taking daily trips to the bank with Monkey so he could see his "girlfriend" and get a treat. Little did he know that Michele was actually bringing a healthy treat and substituting it so he'd have something that was good for him to eat.

Taking the time to get Monkey the proper diagnosis, putting him on the proper medications, tailoring his diet, and of course smothering him in love gave all of us a wonderful seventeen months together. Monkey's little heart finally gave out as he rested in our arms in his home.

During our time with Monkey, Michele and I had discussed starting a dog hospice. Without the support of the community, we were limited to the number of dogs we could save and care for. One day, a few weeks after Monkey's death, Michele told me she had created a Facebook page, "Monkey's House a Dog Hospice & Sanctuary." Michele said she did it for me, and so it began. If Poncho and McKinsey were the sparks and Goldie the kindling, then Monkey was the log creating a raging fire. We were ready to start Monkey's House a Dog Hospice & Sanctuary.

Neither of us had any idea how healing this would be nor how successful Monkey's House would become. Our mission statement reads as follows:

"The mission of Monkey's House is to provide loving care to homeless dogs with terminal diagnoses or hard-to-adopt disabilities. We strive to promote optimum wellness through individually tailored nutrition and exercise in a home setting. All the veterinary care needed for quality of life lived in this peaceful, rural community is provided. Monkey's House is a 501(c)3 nonprofit organization."

In the following chapters, we introduce you to some of our family members, past and present who are living, or have lived out their final and happy days/months/years at Monkey's House immersed in personalized care and surrounded by love. The lives and personalities of these hospice dogs have touched our lives in ways we never could have imagined. We want to share the final chapters of their lives with you.

CHAPTER 2

WELCOME TO THE FAMILY

It truly takes a community to run and make Monkey's House a success. A while ago, I wanted to come up with a different term for the words *community* or *village* as they seem to be thrown around like beads at Mardi Gras. Think about it: How many times have you heard the term *community* or the saying, "It takes a village"? I was looking for a word that expressed a true commitment. In my search for the ultimate word, I pondered a few terms but ended up ruling out words such as *tribe*, a little on the wild side, doesn't quite fit our senior hospice dogs; *hamlet* sounds dignified, kind of Shakespearian, probably a better fit for an English bulldog rescue; and *kinship* brought to mind feuds like those between the Hatfields and McCoys. We want our dogs to live in harmony. Therefore, after much deliberation, my chosen word was *family*.

Since you are reading this book, I'd consider you part of our family, the Monkey's House *family*. I love this word and have been using it to describe our volunteers, fosters, supporters, and contributors. Sure, you can be in a community but members of a family are closer-knit, have deeper connections to your cause, and are committed to helping you succeed. I hope that your personal families are close, too, but from my own experience, they can be challenging. Thankfully, the only challenging part of the Monkey's House family is pulling together to save and care for hospice dogs—a family minus the drama.

AUNTS AND UNCLES

We've coined the terms "aunts" and "uncles" for our volunteers. To really get to know a dog's wants and needs, you need to be more than a volunteer, you need to be a family member like an aunt or uncle to these dogs. We have well over fifty aunts and uncles, about twenty come to the house on a regular basis. Monkey's House is unique as it is in our home, not a facility. We want the dogs to live in a family environment.

As in any dog sanctuary, there is a long list of chores that need to be completed each day. The normal mundane but necessary things like doing laundry, cleaning floors, working in the yard, and restocking supplies seem to be nonstop. In fact, our industrial washing machine runs at least three time a day because of all the bedding we go through. Throw in the mix we're a hospice where dogs have major medical issues, which adds quite a bit of complexity to our days. Besides the normal activities like walking and bathing, many of the dogs need one-on-one attention when it comes to eating. You may see Aunt Trish sitting on the floor next to Cole, a seventy-pound Lab mix, spoon-feeding him. When that fails, you have to toss the spoon and dip your hand right into the food; eight out of ten times that will do the trick. A little persistence and a mushy hand gets the prize! We don't feed our dogs Kibble, only gently cooked or raw food. We have developed great relationships with many of our residents through hand-feeding.

The aunts and uncles love all the dogs, but I can see that many have favorites. You can probably attest to the fact that we all have preferences for big or small dogs or for particular breeds. Aunt Terry prefers the larger dogs; to no surprise, she's also a member of Brookline Labrador Retriever Rescue. Michele met her years ago when she was a Brookline volunteer. The past couple of years, we welcomed a few of their Labs with terminal illnesses into Monkey's House.

Aunt Tracey has been with us since 2015 and she's a "smalls" magnet. Tracey was kind enough to write this passage on her love of the little ones at Monkey's House.

FOR THE LOVE OF "SMALLS"

"What is it about small dogs that makes me fall head over heels in love with them? Is it their tiny but strong-willed nature? Or how each one is overly adorable? Or the fact that they give so much? Maybe it's all of the above. Whatever the reason, I seem to be drawn to them.

Nothing compares to walking through the Monkey's House door and having a pint-sized pup greet you. The tail wagging, talking, body language could not be clearer. They are just as happy to see me as I am to see them. They are so affectionate and act as though you are the center of their universe. I immediately have a huge smile on my face and it remains throughout my visit.

The bond that I have formed with some of the "littles" at Monkey's House has been incredible. Lil, Bea, Penny, and Maisey have all stolen a huge piece of my heart. I instantly felt connected to each one as if we were meant to meet and be in each other's lives. The love runs deep, and I have cherished every moment spent with them.

I miss those that have crossed the Rainbow Bridge. I miss our cuddles and kisses. I miss their big personalities. But I have lots of fond memories and will forever hold each one close to my heart. I know there will be more tiny ones that I will love, and I'm grateful for that. There's more than enough room in this mushy heart of mine.

Thank you, Monkey's House, for allowing me to love your smallest residents. My heart will always remain open for business. I like having this smile on my face ... it feels good."

THE TRANSFORMATION OF BEA

It's not just Tracey's love of the "smalls" but also the love they express toward her that is beautiful to behold. She makes a soulful connection with them in what seems like a blink of an eye. Out of the four that she mentioned—Lil, Bea, Penny, and Maisey— I believe the one that grabbed her heart the most was a little Chihuahua named Bea. I don't know if Tracey could tell you why this once-broken little angel took flight with her heart, but she surely did.

Throughout the years at Monkey's House, I've noticed some of the aunts have a special attraction to those dogs that were truly broken, both body and soul. Bea was one of those totally broken dogs when she came here. A week after Bea arrived, I was with Tracey in our family room when Bea started to have convulsions. As I calmly picked her up, holding her close to my body, I realized this was the first time Tracey witnessed a dog having a seizure at Monkey's House. Your first time seeing a seizure can be very traumatic; the most important thing to remember is to stay calm. I wonder if this incident created an even stronger bond between Tracey and Bea.

Like so many others that have made their way to Monkey's House, this little, old, sick dog was about to be killed. Kimberly Price Astringer from Tiny Paws Rescue saw her, contacted us, and thankfully Bea made her way into our family. Sadly, older sick dogs have very little chance of ever leaving a shelter alive unless there's someone willing to advocate for them.

The first order of business was to get her a new name. Her surrender form listed her name as Kimbar, but that just didn't fit her. She needed a name that would bring some youthful energy and spunk into her life. The name of Beyoncé was chosen, but we ended up calling her Bea.

Bea was blind and deaf, had severe dental disease, a nasty hernia, a dislocated hip, and bad knees. She was barely able to eat with her painful teeth, and what little nutrition that made it into her body was being drained by tapeworms. The goal was to do everything in our power to get her broken body well enough to enjoy life. Our promise to Bea was that there would be lots and lots of love in her time with us. We surely kept that promise.

Aunt Tracey doted on Bea at our home, out by our pond, and even took her on picnics to local parks. On many sunny days, Tracey would pull up to the house ready to take Bea on an adventure. I always imagined that one day Tracey would pull up in a convertible so Bea could feel the sun on her face as the wind blew through her hair, those giant ears flapping in the wind. We could have changed the title of the hit movie, *The Art of Racing in the Rain*, to *The Art of Basking in the Sun* and have Bea as the star. Bea and Aunt Tracey were soul mates, no doubt about it. If you saw them together, you would agree.

Bea and Aunt Tracey, soul mates.

Transformation is a powerful word, even more so when you see it take place in a completely broken dog like Bea. She was a remarkable dog, and to watch her transform was nothing short of amazing; I liken it to a miracle. To have seen this little one strut her stuff day after day brought all of us such joy. Bea didn't just have a strong will to live, she thrived in her environment. On any given day, she would explore the entire downstairs and never allowed her being blind and deaf get in her way. It's pretty incredible just how aware she really was. She had an attitude, too; no doubt this played a role in her ability to adapt so well. She loved to "talk" and would cuddle up next to any other dog. Bea enjoyed every day— not bad for a dog that was a half hour from being put down at a local kill shelter.

Shortly after joining us, Bea suffered multiple, "hard to break" seizures; we believe she had a brain tumor on top of everything else. While her seizures were quite challenging, they didn't stop her from living life to the fullest.

Bea passed gently in the arms of her beloved Aunt Tracey two years after joining us at Monkey's House. She was spared from becoming one of our country's sad statistics. Her family of sixteen years disposed of her at a kill shelter. A dog that old and sick never stood a chance had it not been for Kimberly, her guardian angel. Bea defied the odds and led a beautiful last chapter of her life.

We are often asked about quality of life issues and knowing when it's time to assist the dogs to the Rainbow Bridge. If you had only read Bea's diagnosis that I outlined, you might have wondered what kind of life was possible for her. Anyone who saw our Facebook posts about Bea never would have guessed she had so many ailments. For a dog who hadn't known much kindness, a clean soft bed, regular meals, veterinary care, an occasional bath, and being carried outside—these are really simple needs, and we didn't have to resort to extraordinary means to satisfy them—her quality of life was great.

Evaluating quality of life is a heavy burden. We remember our dogs when they were young, chasing a ball or running with a Frisbee. Bea came to us very late in life and very damaged. We fixed what we could for her. We loved her for who she was. We gave her all the belly rubs she demanded, and the heavy burden was lifted. We felt sure she was happy with her life at Monkey's House.

MINI-MONKEY'S HOUSES

We have some aunts and uncles that take a different path in becoming part of the Monkey's House family; they are our *fosters*. Fosters are a critical necessity for every shelter or rescue to be successful; there's no exception here. We have *quarantine fosters* and *forever fosters*. The names pretty much sum up what they do.

Since our house is home to more or less twenty-five dogs at any given time, we have to be diligent at keeping pathogens from making their way onto our property. Most of our dogs have weakened immune systems, and we don't want to put them at risk by bringing in a contagion from outside of Monkey's House. This is where our quarantine fosters come into play. When it's determined a dog meets our criteria, plus we have space available, the next critical task is to get a foster that will take the dog for a minimum of two weeks, maybe more if it develops something like *kennel cough* (also known as canine infectious tracheobronchitis is a highly contagious respiratory disease.) Thankfully, we've had great luck finding fosters for that quarantine period. We've never had to turn a dog away for that reason.

The other type of foster, the *forever foster*, is much like a forever family member except Monkey's House supports them in every way and has say over the care the dog receives. We've developed a very good hospice program that has proven itself time and time again; we want to ensure all our dogs, even those not physically living at our home, reap the benefits of our high standards.

Generally, our forever fosters take one dog into their family; they may also have a personal dog of their own. We do have some fosters that take more than one; for example, Aunt Holly generally has three. However, it always seems she ends up with the cutest dogs. I always offer to bring one or two back to our house, but she won't give them up!

With the success we've had with Monkey's House, I've been asked many times, "What's the plan?" Basically, they are asking us if we have plans to expand. The key to saving and caring for more hospice dogs is twofold: first, our mission is to show folks they can care for a hospice dog at home; second, we hope to expand our forever foster family program to give us the opportunity to save more dogs. We have a very dedicated group that does a wonderful job supporting the pups in the program. The dogs in forever foster join us on all our field trips and even take photos with Santa. We are really one big, happy family.

OUR GLOBAL FAMILY

When I think back, say twenty-five years ago when Michele and I had a "normal" life, we would have dinner and discuss how our days went, mine at the office and hers in the hospital. I always found hers more interesting than my bits-and-bytes computer issues. One story she told me stands out to this day.

As a nurse, you need to sign off on all surgeries your patients are scheduled to undergo, basically saying they are in good-enough health to have their procedures. On one occasion, Michele was explaining to me that her patient needed to have brain surgery, and she was asked to sign off to say he was ready; she refused. Michele was working at a local hospital at the time, and this would have been only the second brain surgery procedure the hospital performed. She asked why her patient wasn't being transferred across the river to one of the excellent hospitals in Philadelphia less than fifteen miles away. She took the hit that day standing by her principles, and more importantly, her patient. Michele's philosophy was and always will be, "It's all about the patient," human or dog.

I told this story to show the commitment Michele has for a life and that we started Monkey's House to give dogs a good last chapter of their lives. Most important, Monkey's House started out to be, and still is, all about the dogs. I'm not sure if we were just so focused on being able to give hospice dogs a great ending to their lives or what, but an amazing thing happened on our journey that we hadn't anticipated. We gained a family—a supportive family that spans the globe.

We had never imagined that the Monkey's House Facebook page would become a platform for not only our daily posts but also an avenue for many to express their emotions about the loss of a best friend or adopting a senior dog with medical issues. A family has grown and is very supportive to all who take part.

MLBOB—A FEISTY BEAGLE THAT LOVED PEANUT BUTTER PIES

In the summer of 2016, we brought in a very special little beagle that was dearly loved by our aunts and uncles as well as our Monkey's House family. When this little fellow passed, the overwhelming response was astounding with over a thousand well-wishers showing their sympathy via Facebook. These were not your typical "RIPs" that you might normally see, but paragraphs on what this little beagle had meant to them, these individuals who only knew him through social media by reading about his antics and looking at those pictures of his soulful eyes.

MLBob was called Mr. Bean at the shelter; however, his quarantine foster mom Aunt Dawn felt he was more of a Bob. Bob earned the name Feisty Bob when he tried to bite one of our veterinarians, Dr. Anthony, and needed to be muzzled. We have only had three Monkey's House pups earn that distinction. Aunt Dawn told us he was quite the character and to be ready for one spicy little guy.

When he physically joined us at the house a few weeks later, he was potty trained and no longer jumping on chairs to climb onto the dining room table. At that point, Michele said he needed a name to keep his mischief to a minimum. His name was changed from Feisty Bob to Relaxed Bob. You may be wondering what's up with the name MLBob. Well, through his antics, many faces, and charm, his Facebook family demanded his name be changed once more to Much Loved Bob, also known as MLB or MLBob. (I would like to point out that he was deaf so he didn't mind the name change as long as he had his choice of foods.)

The hospice dogs that come through our door have a host of terminal aliments. As you would expect, some are in worse shape than others, and MLBob appeared to be one of the worst cases. He was filled with cancer and was retaining fluids in his abdomen. He was a cute, tiny beagle with a swollen belly and the biggest soulful eyes I've ever seen. The shelter veterinarian estimated he had a month to live; after the three weeks at Aunt Dawn's house, this meant his time should have been very limited at Monkey's House.

MLBob fit in rather quickly and was making friends with the other residents. Some of his special snuggle buddies were Bea and of course Lucy and Mr. Peebody, the other beagles in the house. At one point, the beagles had a bow-wow and discussed changing the name of Monkey's House to Beagleville, but that was quickly squashed by the Chihuahuas, the real muscle in the dog world. The pitty and shepherd mixes we had at the house had nothing on these six-pound pups that think they are sixty pounds of tough!

MLBob with his "peanut butter pie, please" face.

One of MLBob's favorite things in life was peanut butter pies, and his Aunt Dawn would buy them freshly made just for him from a local pet bakery. In the beginning, he was a very picky eater, and the pies were the only thing he would eat. We were thankful we could get anything into his belly. At Monkey's House, we pride ourselves on our approach to nutrition, using fresh and holistic food therapy, but at times you just need to get food down the hatch. We followed these food rules with MLBob for as long as we could, but eventually we decided healthy food wasn't going to keep him alive. He would create his "pizza, please" face or a "Cheerios, please" face; he even had a "pancakes, please" face. He was okay with pizza for breakfast and pancakes for dinner. So all rules were broken as they were all yummy to him.

When we thought MLBob was nearing the end, Michele contacted our aunts and uncles, notifying them to come and say their good-byes. At that point, his stomach was extremely enlarged and he was not eating; he was clearly slipping away. Aunt Dawn quickly arrived, bringing with her a container of chicken nuggets. When the dogs are preparing to go to the Rainbow Bridge, healthy eating requirements are off the table. Whatever food they love, even junk food, is permitted.

MLBob ate all the nuggets. Through the night and into the wee hours of the morning, a small miracle occurred. As we woke, there was MLBob standing with a stomach that was almost normal strolling around the family room. He was still full of cancer, but those magical nuggets helped drain his stomach and gave him an additional four months to enjoy life. He went on field trips and had a little wagon he would ride in we called "Waggin' One." This wagon allowed him to join the others at the state park or just around the farm. He loved the sun in his face; he loved life.

In nine months, Much Loved Bob had created a whole new life for himself and had gathered up pieces of all of our hearts. He left this world peacefully and without pain with his foster mom Aunt Dawn and Michele at his side. He could not have been more loved. We were extremely saddened but will be forever grateful that we had time to show him love and a kinder side of humanity. Much Loved Bob stole everyone's heart with his "faces," his antics, and his peanut butter pies.

While the end of a life is sad, it would have been a far greater loss to have never had him in our lives. Thanks to those who let him steal their hearts and for loving him along with us, he finished living life to his fullest ability, not as a poor, sick, homeless dog that would have been a statistic. Instead he passed as Much Loved Bob, gently on the softest blanket we had, on a chair overlooking the yard and pond at the place he loved and called home. He was wrapped in a blanket covered in hearts and gently laid in his final resting place with a peanut butter pie.

As for the thousand comments, there's one that I would like to share, what I call a tribute to Much Loved Bob by Betty Woody:

> *"There was something about MLBob that touched hearts in every corner of this country. Maybe it was those huge, liquid eyes that silently spoke a thousand words? Maybe it was his quirky behavior or his fragile little body? Or could it have been his endless menus of delightful baked goods? It was probably a little of all of that.*
>
> *But you know what I really think it was? I think we all found a piece of ourselves in this little fellow's journey.*
>
> *MLBob probably wasn't the prettiest or the sweetest dog that ever lived at Monkey's House. He wasn't the strongest or most unique. In another life, he might have been that dog we pass by in the street without a second glance. On the surface, MLBob was average. Just like most of us appear to be.*
>
> *But because you loved him and believed in him and were willing to invest the time and energy it took to get below the surface and find what lies beneath, we all came to know MLBob as someone extraordinary.*
>
> *Inside that tiny little body beat the heart of a warrior who fought on long after his battle was supposed to end. And I believe he did this because of all of you. He didn't want to leave a life that was perfect beyond his wildest dreams.*

Your love gave MLBob the will to live. And your love assured him it was ok to go."

I am thankful for the inspiration of our global family. At times we get emotionally overwhelmed. Reading uplifting comments on social media and letters of support encourage us to push through the difficult times and carry on. There are always more dogs to save.

THE RESCUE COMMUNITY

There is a vast array of dog rescue organizations, and thankfully the community is fairly close-knit. The number-one goal is the well-being of the dogs, and in general, all the organizations work well together. Monkey's House has a great relationship with many of the groups. Since we are one of only a few hospice sanctuaries, Michele gets many inquiries asking for her expert advice on dogs with major medical issues. Most rescues don't have the expertise to deal with special-needs cases. On many occasions, those dogs may find their way to Monkey's House as we are better equipped to care for their particular circumstances.

In working together, wonderful things can and do happen. Take Betty, for example, the dog I talk about in chapter 6, "Home for the Holidays." Her rescue story started at the Animal Care and Control Team of Philadelphia (aka ACCT) and eventually to the loving home of Vicki and Fred. On one of Kimberly Price Astringer's many visits to ACCT, she noticed Betty and messaged Michele. After discussing her diagnosis, it was determined we could take her. Kathy McGuire from NJ Aid for Animals pulled and transported her to our house ("pulled" or "pulling" translates to adopting the dog, paying the fee, and signing the contract that states it is going to a rescue). While Betty was busy stealing our hearts, we found out she really wasn't a hospice case and could be adopted into a forever family. Then, through the help of Dawn Hullings (cofounder of One Love Animal Rescue), Betty was transferred from her rescue to the home of an incredible foster mom, Vicki Watkins.

You're probably saying this must be an extreme case, that it can't take this many kind-hearted people and organizations to save a dog. This is more the norm than the exception. I left out all the volunteers who run these organizations and do the day-to-day activities. Of course, none of this would even be possible without the generosity of donors. It takes a small army willing to get their hands dirty or open their wallets to save a Betty, or a Bailey, or even perhaps your dog.

SORA—MICHELE'S SOUL MATE

In talking about our Monkey's House family, which includes aunts and uncles, fosters, and our global community, I have to add in one other member that has made a huge impact on Monkey's House—our personal dog, Sora.

Michele found her soul mate when she rescued Sora back in 2013. We had recently lost our dog, Poncho, a little dog that never left Michele's side, her true companion. Although we had other dogs, Michele was heartbroken and eventually began looking to rescue again. After a visit to the local shelter, she came home and told me she thought she found "the" dog. Thing was, it was not Sora but another dog farther down the row of cages. She told me she had passed by a German shepherd that was so sad that she wouldn't even look up as Michele approached her cage. I don't know what went through Michele's head that night, but the next day she came back with that German shepherd and she named her Sora. I wanted to share this piece Michele wrote about Sora:

> "In the fall of 2012, I went on what I thought was a selfish search for a dog for myself. At the time, we had six rescue dogs with physical and emotional limitations that needed us. I wanted a dog that didn't need me, that was well enough to take on adventures that could help me with the foster dogs, (a dog) that I could just enjoy life with. This search took over six months. During this journey where I thought I was just looking for a dog, I was shocked at how much I learned about myself as well as about

dogs. My selfish decision was the best move I ever made. I adopted Sora from a local shelter. I gave her a name, a collar, and a bath. That was all I did.

Sora was easy to love and adjusted as we did from being in a reasonably smallish family to being "part of the staff" as her home welcomed over eighty dogs during her time here. She was my best friend and greatest teacher. She helped all of the dogs feel safe and grow confident. She taught me the difference from acting calm (I thought that was the absence of screaming) and actually being calm. She showed me how my actions, my posture, and my voice affected every dog here. They all respected her yet she was quiet, almost subdued. She made it look easy. She was a huge part of the quiet and Zen feeling everyone experiences here. I promise to honor her by maintaining the

Sora, the Zen master of Monkey's House.

uniqueness of a regular home with twenty-five-plus dogs living together in a sense of quiet that is almost blissful.

Sora accompanied the other pups on vet visits and adventures. She waited patiently and selflessly on the long days we would spend at the vet's while a pup, or five, had surgery. She was a gentle soul who loved all of us and whose presence is greatly missed.

I'm wondering if Bea was accidentally stepped on by one of our bigger guys at the Rainbow Bridge and a royal ruckus ensued. Sora will do an excellent job keeping peace, and perhaps she was just simply needed more there.

I've learned many times over that we don't die of a broken heart. Although it feels like an impossible burden to carry her loss, she was worth all of that part. It doesn't go away, but over time we adjust to the pain and the absence of her presence. And of course, I pray we will be together again someday.

Sora, twenty-five years with you would not have been long enough. Thank you for sharing almost six years with us. We will love you forever."

CHAPTER 3

WHAT DO GEORGE CLOONEY AND MARY POPPINS HAVE IN COMMON?

Reaching home after a very long commute, I take a deep sigh of relief; I finally get to see the family and hear how their day went. Coming down the driveway, I pass Waggin' One, our bus that not only takes the pups to the veterinary clinic but also is our "fun mobile" for all our field trips. Looks like it's parked for a quick getaway to maybe another great excursion to the beach or park. Michele and the crew wouldn't be sneaking out for a midweek getaway without me, now would they?

Next, I notice the Cottage with its little front yard surrounded by a white picket fence. By now, my demeanor has changed as I feel a small smile start to form on my face; the stress of my day seems to be dissolving. The Cottage reminds me of a small home you'd see in a village nestled in the English countryside. Only this cottage is inhabited by dogs. In the yard is a red-and-white striped umbrella, abundant potted flowers, and a colorful wind spinner that's catching a light breeze at the moment.

As I park the car, it's decision time: Do I take a step to the left and head into the house, or a step to the right and head to the Cottage? In the house, I know I'll be in for an exciting greeting. At a minimum, half a dozen dogs will be waiting at the door. Upon entering, I'll quickly kneel down and stretch my arms wide to pet as many dogs as possible. If I close my eyes, I can almost imagine I'm touching angels in heaven. There will even be a few that demand I pick them up for a hug as they give me a kiss on the cheek—no Frenchies, please! It's also an opportunity to say hello to Michele and see how her day went. Decision made—it's into the house.

As I take that step toward the house, I happen to glance over my right shoulder. At that moment, a nose is protruding between the pickets of the Cottage fence. That little black nose, a stark contrast from the white pickets, looks familiar. It's Shark's nose, the cutest little beagle you've ever seen. Quickly, I pivot to the right and change course; today, it's the Cottage. That cute little pup changed my decision. Like a firefly to a light, I hasten my step. The first pups to see Dad this evening will be the Cottage crew.

Shark must have alerted Shadow as she came out to greet me, too. With their faces pushing against the gate, I carefully open it, pushing them back just enough to let me squeeze through while making sure there are no escapees. They are right on my heels as we walk along the path and into the Cottage. This section of the house is quite different from the main house, not in furnishings or style; it is just more laid-back than the house is. I joke and say these pups have taken over my "man cave."

Shadow, a black Lab mix, climbs up onto a comfy sofa in the Healing Room. The room is lined with large windows on both sides, and during the day healing sunlight engulfs the room, thus its name. I plop myself down next to Shadow and start stroking her silky black coat. Pop music is coming from their radio in the den, the other room that makes up the Cottage. I know that's Shark's station as he's the hipster. Shadow is mellower; I'd take her for a jazz or classical enthusiast. Little Shark wanders over, and I get the impression he's saying, "Hey, Dude, you have two hands, pet me, too." I happily oblige.

SHARK—MY DANCING BUDDY

Rarely do we know the history of the dogs that are lucky enough to make their way to Monkey's House. What we can tell you about Shark T. Beagle, his proper name, is that he had a hard life that led to both physical and mental concerns. Physically, he has heart and kidney issues that are being treated with diet and medication. Our biggest fear is his spine; he has an old spinal injury that affects the way he walks. Two of Shark's vertebrae are completely compressed. His pain is controlled through pain management. However, we have been told this old back injury will leave him paralyzed at some point in his life. The goal is to delay that as long as possible and make sure he lives pain-free.

Because of the way he was treated in his prior life, along with his back injury, Shark distrusted people when he first came here. He wouldn't let anybody touch him from the neck back. Heaven forbid if you did; he would react like a rabid dog, like something out of a Stephen King movie. He has come a long way in the past two years, during which I've become

his best bud. There isn't a day that goes by that I'm not working with Shark in some capacity, showing him that people aren't so bad. I use a nontraditional method that I designed that fits his personality. I call it the "dance and touch" method. (Thinking back, maybe I learned this when Michele and I were dating, but I digress.)

Shark likes his pop music, so I squat down and dance, petting his face, neck, and then running my hands down his body. He loves the face and ear rubs, toler-ates the light body touching. He

Shark looking for a dance partner.

even enjoys dancing with me as he'll take little choppy steps and spin in circles. He's gaining trust daily and has made a huge change, almost 180 degrees since the time he arrived.

Shark wears a harness like most of our dogs (harnesses gives us greater control over a dog while preventing injuries to their neck or trachea.) Although it's the proper size, he often seems to get a leg out of it. That's when I hear one of the aunts saying, "Where's Jeff? Shark needs help with his harness." I think, "Yikes!" Remember, I said he almost had a 180-degree change; he can still be very finicky when it comes to the harness. He trusts me the most and will tolerate quite a bit from me, thus it's "Jeff's job." About 90 percent of the time, I can get the harness fixed in about five to ten minutes. It involves some dancing, petting, and wrangling but eventually all is well with the world. The other 10 percent of the time I can get it off but can't get it back on; he's going naked until he forgets about it or I get up the nerve for another go. I treasure my fingers!

Walks are one of Shark's favorite activities, and he goes on all our field trips. He can't be picked up because of his back, nor would you want to try because of his teeth! But he'll walk right up the steps of Waggin' One and we'll load him into a floor-level crate by tossing a treat into the back of the crate. He'll head for the goody as we shut the door quickly. I guess we can say Shark self-loads! If we ever do need to carry him, we carry him in his crate.

We have all heard the horrors of laboratory beagles; we believe that might have been Shark's previous life. He's one of the smallest beagles we have ever seen, and he had never been in a house before he was rescued. You might think he sounds like a hunting dog, and I would agree except that he was debarked. Plus, we've had half a dozen hunting beagles, and they were all extremely friendly and actually sought out attention, unlike Shark when he first arrived.

Devocalization, also known as *debarking*, can be done surgically; however, we also know many of these procedures are not performed by a veterinarian; they are done by someone shoving a pipe-like object down the dog's throat. Besides having to endure the agony of this cruel procedure, it strips dogs of their natural ability to vocalize and communicate.

Shark initially started out in the house with the other dogs but eventually became very protective of not only his food but also his beds or whatever else he felt belonged to him. Once he was moved to the Cottage, most of these guarding issues were resolved, but to this day we can't touch his food bowl!

You may be wondering how we determine which dogs reside in the Cottage besides those with guarding issues like Shark's. With around twenty-five dogs at our home, you can only imagine the array of personalities. In a lot of ways, dogs are very much like us—some are extroverts, others introverts. They either do well interacting with a large group of dogs or they don't. We also have their physical ailments to consider. We had a blind yellow Lab named Blaze that loved being in the house with us; however, he eventually got tired of being banged into from other smaller blind and deaf pups roaming the house. It was like a pinball machine; you would see the little guys walking around using their noses to navigate through smell and touch, bumping into everything. Blaze didn't appreciate being used as one of their pinball bumpers, so we moved him into the Cottage and he would just visit the house.

SHADOW, FROM "CHAINED" TO MOBILE

Unlike Shark's past, we do know a little about Shadow's prior life; she had been permanently tethered in someone's backyard. That's what we refer to as a "chain dog." Sadly, Shadow was not the first chain dog we've taken in and probably not the last. She arrived here three-legged; she could not bear any weight on her right front leg. If it was physically possible, she would have been two-legged, only walking on her back legs as the other front leg was not in much better shape.

The Humane Society looks upon continuous confinement of a dog by a tether as inhumane and so do we. Continuous tethering significantly restricts a dog's movement, and as we all know, dogs are naturally social beings who thrive on interaction with humans and other dogs. They are genetically predisposed to living in a pack setting. A dog kept chained alone in one spot like Shadow had been generally suffers immense psychological damage. In Shadow's case, it also led to her physical problems. She became neurotic, unhappy, and obsessed with chewing her front legs. The one thing those nasty chains couldn't do was diminish her desire to be loved and give love.

When she arrived at Monkey's House, both of her front legs were raw; in a few spots, the skin was completely gone and the muscle was exposed. But as bad as that looked and surely stung, that was not the reason for her being lame. After consults with many specialists, it was determined that the bones themselves were deformed. Early on, it appeared the only option available was to remove her right leg, which would make Shadow a *tripod dog*. Dogs *can* thrive on three legs; however, we had doubts about the strength of her other front leg and if she could put any weight on it since it wasn't a normal, healthy leg.

We continued to try different treatments hoping to find the right solution for Shadow. Michele persevered and found the magic combination of treatments. On a weekly basis, Michele and Aunt Nancy load up Waggin' One with whomever is heading in for veterinary appointments that day. Shadow has a standing appointment for an underwater treadmill workout followed by cold laser therapy. This, along with food therapy and medication, has changed Shadow's life. She's become much stronger and has been given the gift of mobility with much less pain. While her legs are not completely healed, a dog that came here three-legged is now running up the steps of the bus.

Shadow is more persuasive with her dramatic eyes than a little girl asking her dad for an ice cream cone or for another ride at the carnival. She gives her aunts that look, and the next thing you know, Aunt Terry is taking her out for a back-road excursion. When she's really on her game, she gets Aunt Trudy to take her to the local park for a change of scenery. For the finale, they stop at Arby's for a roast beef sandwich (hold the bread, please!). I have to admit, not just the aunts fall for those eyes; I can't resist them either. At times when I'm walking her, she pulls me right to Waggin' One and up the steps she goes. More

Shadow and I after a drive around the neighborhood in Waggin' One.

than once, I had to come back in the house, grab the bus keys, and tell Michele we were taking a little excursion. After a quick jolt round the country block, she would unload with what I swear was a smile. She had her own trip with her dad.

Shadow loves children. Aunt Claire's granddaughter, Camryn, will accompany her grandmother to Monkey's House on occasion when there's a school break. Camryn loves to sit on the couch with Shadow and read her a story. I don't think it mattered what Camryn was reading, it could have been Dr. Seuss's *Cat in the Hat*, Shadow thought it was a literary masterpiece. I saw an article once about children reading to shelter dogs at the Humane Society of Missouri, their Shelter Buddies Reading Program. Research shows reading has a calming effect on the animals while nurturing empathy in children. Shadow certainly seemed to enjoy it.

Shadow does very well in the Cottage with Shark and just about any other dog that pays them a visit. She thrives in a tranquil setting with less activity and fewer dogs. Being chained alone for all those years makes her anxious when she is around a large group of dogs.

We also have to make sure other dogs don't bang into her legs because they are still very sensitive to touch. But what continues to amaze us about Shadow and about each and every dog we bring in that's been abused is despite their mistreatment, their passion and devotion to us is emotionally overwhelming. Witnessing this over and over, you would think Michele and I wouldn't give it a second thought; but we do, and we cherish their spirit and desire for affection.

I tell Shark and Shadow it's time for me to head into the house as Mom's going to wonder what happened to me. As I step into the garage heading toward the main house, I notice George Clooney with six big boxes full of Allprovide dog food next to him. (Allprovide is very supportive of Monkey's House donating 60 pounds of food per week.) Bet you didn't know that George is a regular at Monkey's House. He's always working, keeps the food fresh and very appetizing to look at. "Ok George, let's get this food put away," I say.

The extra-large freezer that was graciously donated to us by Minus Forty is named George Clooney. Not sure if Michele or one of the aunts came up with that name. It is a very good-looking freezer and so functional, that's the key. Minus Forty even went the extra mile and illuminated the Monkey's House logo across the top. I'm okay with it being named after George; he did adopt a senior dog named Einstein, and from what I've read, he's a dog lover and supports the rescue community. I just need him to come for a visit and stand next to his twin—now that would be a great photo-op!

After loading 150 pounds of raw food into George, I finally head into the house to see the rest of the furry family and Michele. As I enter the laundry room, I notice the closet door is open, and I see our magical nanny in the closet—Mary Poppins, that is. She lives at Monkey's House and helps sustains life through her suitcase full of tricks. Well, at least that's what Michele has named the crash cart that contains an oxygen concentrator and other emergency supplies. She thought the term "crash cart" didn't suit a hospice, and a key factor in Michele's mind was not to scare the aunts and uncles, so the name Mary Poppins fit the bill. In emergencies, the number-one rule is to stay calm so you can take appropriate actions. Who's better to bring comfort measures to a dog than Mary Poppins and her magic?

By now, you might be thinking we are a little eccentric about names. I swear that we have a purpose behind our madness when it comes to names, except for maybe George Clooney. Many of the dogs we take in don't have names that fit their personalities—or should I say the names don't have the "aura" we would like them to have. If the dog can hear and respond to its name, we won't change it. However, a good portion of our dogs are deaf, so we are free to get creative.

Michele once told me her approach to naming a dog really depends on what we want that dog to aspire to. If a dog appears weak, she will think of an empowering name; a hyper dog will get a name that exudes calmness. Generally, the name comes to her quickly, or she might ask an aunt or uncle for a suggestion. Below are a few examples of the names some of the dogs were given when they came to Monkey's House:

- Mr. Peebody: The original name for this old hunting beagle that would pee on anything and anybody was Hammer. I remember the first few days after he arrived; an aunt came into the house after walking him telling us he peed on her leg like it was a fire hydrant! There was an uproar of laughter from the other folks in the house when they heard this as this wasn't a first. That was the defining moment when he earned his name. Sometimes, you just have to laugh and roll with the punches.

- Princess Granny: She arrived with the name Granny. Now, who doesn't or didn't love their granny, but we wanted to give her a little more dignity and grace, so we added Princess.

- Joey: A pit bull who needed a personality. Michele changed his name from Blue to Joey as in Joey Tribbiani from the sitcom *Friends*. One of dog Joey's favorite things to do is close his eyes, put his nose up, and just smell the air. We can only imagine what he is smelling. If you watched *Friends*, you might remember that the character Joey was an actor, and when he landed a job on a soap opera, he learned a new and overly dramatic acting technique by drawing out the time it took to speak his lines to make them sound more mysterious or cliffhanger-like. He called it "smelling the fart" acting, and he worked hard at mastering it. Our Joey is a natural; look out, soap operas!

- Lil: The smallest dog to call Monkey's House home, weighing in at just four pounds. Michele's great-grandmother came from Finland. She was a very strong woman and her nickname was Lil. We wanted that strength for our little Lil, too.

- Holly: When Liz from Liz's Rescue Wagon delivered this German shepherd mix to us, she didn't have a name. Liz asked if she could name her because she had a feeling about a name that would suit her. Liz said her travels took her though a small, quaint town called Mt. Holly, and she felt the name Holly fit her well. We agreed.

- LA: Michele was in LA appearing on the *Hallmark Channel's Home & Family* show when she received a call asking her if Monkey's House had room for another dog. The name LA fit her as she was quite the star.

LEO THE LION

One of my favorite names given to one of our dogs was Leo, as in *Leo the Lion —King of the Jungle*. Leo was found by a good samaritan out taking a walk. As she passed a dumpster, she noticed what she thought was a dirty old rag someone intended to toss in the container but missed. Wanting to keep her neighborhood tidy, she went to pick it up, only to her surprise it wasn't a rag at all but an unrecognizable dog. He was covered in dirt and grime, and she noticed he had a gash on his head that was grossly infected, apparently from blunt-force trauma. She quickly wrapped him up and took him to the Voorhees

Animal Orphanage. After spending some time to heal at the shelter, he was given to the loving foster parents, Laurie and Raf, who cared for him for another month while he continued his recuperation. Then he was brought to Monkey's House to start his next chapter.

By the time he came to Monkey's House, Leo's head wound had healed, although he had an array of physical and psychological issues. For starters, he was blind and deaf, had kidney failure, and what we believed was the worst case of PTSD that we had ever seen. He was so scared, when you went to pick him up, he would almost jump out of his skin. It was heartbreaking to see this little shih tzu flinch every time anyone touched him. Our work was cut out for us, to make him feel safe and loved for the first time in his life.

The days turned into weeks, weeks into months, and two miraculous things took place with Leo. First, his kidney failure was first managed and then slowed with food therapy; and second, Leo was starting to get used to being touched. All in all, it took a good year for our little Leo to gain his courage, much like the Cowardly Lion in the *Wizard of Oz*. He initially enjoyed the company of the other dogs, snuggling with big or small, LA or Lil. Eventually, he loved

Leo, our brave little lion.

being gently picked up and put on one of the aunt's laps. Seems like every time I would see Aunt Trudy, she would have both Leo and Josie, another shih tzu, on her lap together. The little dog that at one point had no reason to have faith in mankind now trusts everything that happens here is good.

Sally Morgan has visited us a few times. She's a physical therapist with specialties in craniosacral therapist (a gentle, hands-on approach that releases tensions deep in the body to relieve pain and dysfunction and improve whole-body health and performance), and TTouch (focuses on healing, positive animal training, and communication). She's extremely popular with the pups and has worked on Leo a few times. We are fascinated at what an impact this noninvasive and gentle treatment has on his physical and mental well-being.

One night, Michele told me a funny story about Leo.

"Leo generated an entire load of laundry, the need for an emergency bath for himself, and a complete wardrobe change for me. He eats with the gusto of a young teenager in a pie-eating contest, but he actually gets very little down the hatch. He has the will to live and make the most of each moment; it's nothing short of amazing. Looking at him, his body has seen better days. But to hold him is an entirely different story. Leo, our little Lion, is very present and fiercely fighting to continue his journey here with us. So, with tears in my eyes, I applaud this little being for spreading dinner everywhere. Go Leo!" Michele stated.

Leo filled his two years with us with love and enjoyment of those special little moments. He made many furry and human friends. He was in two CNN videos, told Santa what he wanted for Christmas, and enjoyed smelling, then peeing, on the seaweed at the Jersey Shore. We couldn't have asked for a better ending for this little "Leo the Lion."

POSITIVE ENERGY

We believe in the power of positive thinking and prayer; both provide energy to the humans who help our dogs transform to be the best they can be to enjoy their final moments. Positive energy is part of the healing process, and it's our responsibility to create and maintain a positive living environment. I just talked about names, not only the dogs' names, but names for appliances, crash carts, and even rooms are meant to promote strength and dignity in a loving and fun atmosphere. We've always felt that way, and in 2019 we attended one of Jack Canfield's seminars, "One Day to Greatness." It reaffirmed our belief in the power of positive thinking.

Jack Canfield firmly believes in the Law of Attraction about which he states, "You will attract into your life whatever you focus on. Whatever you give your energy and attention to will come back to you."

So, if you stay focused on the good and positive things in your life, you will automatically attract better and positive things into your life. If you are focused upon negativity, then that is what will be attracted into your life.

When we focus on the positive aspects of our dogs and how to improve their lives, we are excited, enthusiastic, passionate, and appreciative to be able to serve these dogs. Jack Canfield would say we are sending out positive energy. The Universe, through the Law of Attraction, will respond enthusiastically to these vibrations. The Universe doesn't decide which vibration is better for you, it just responds to whatever energy you are creating, and it gives you more of the same. You get back exactly what you put out there.

We have experienced this time and time again with our global family, praying and having positive thoughts for our dogs in need. We believe this positive energy is one part of the recipe that provides these dogs with the ability to enjoy their final moments, making their final chapters sometimes their best chapters.

CHAPTER 4

WHATEVER IT TAKES

Many of the dogs that come to Monkey's House bring along with them a multitude of issues; facing them is challenging to say the least. However, we do have a large toolbox with both traditional and nontraditional veterinary modalities along with food therapy to help solve or alleviate many of their conditions. Of course, these dogs are hospice, so many of their ailments can't be cured, but that's when we step up our game and get the dogs on the right path to becoming the best they can be. We can't bear looking into their eyes and seeing the sorrow of these broken dogs, let down by the people who were supposed to be there for them. We're thankful they are with us now, the best place possible to live out the remainder of their lives.

Before a new dog arrives, I'll see Michele skimming through medical reports and analyzing blood work results, determining the steps needed to get each dog on the path to wellness based on the diagnosis. She'll schedule a visit with our veterinarian; within a few days of arriving, the dog will be examined and a thorough game plan will be established.

Over the years, we have acquired a top-notch network of veterinarians, including an array of specialists including cardiologists, eye and gastrointestinal specialists, physical therapists, and many others. I can assure you that we use the most skilled and knowledgeable veterinarians in the field; we don't settle for anything less for our dogs. Some of the therapies we have found to be beneficial include the following:

+ Underwater Treadmill—We've used *hydrotherapy* on many of our dogs as it provides a reduced weight-bearing environment and has given our pups many advantages both physically and psychologically. It builds muscle and strength while reducing pain for dogs with arthritic and spinal issues. It also allows those that can no longer walk have the freedom of movement, giving each dog a sense of normalcy.

+ Cold Laser Therapy—is a noninvasive procedure that uses light to stimulate cell regeneration and increase blood circulation. This treatment is also great for dogs with arthritis or joint issues. Our dogs seem to love this treatment as the process releases endorphins. We don't think it hurts that Aunt Beth, who administers the treatment, also has a pocket full of treats!

+ Acupuncture—This ancient Chinese practice uses the placement of tiny needles in energy channels to enhance blood circulation and stimulate the release of hormones with the goal of encouraging the body to correct imbalances. It has helped alleviate many of our dogs' ailments. We generally use this for pain management and arthritis.

+ Regenerative Medicine—*Stem cell therapy* uses the body's own cells to regenerate and heal injured tissue, decrease inflammation, stimulate new blood supply, and stimulate healing and tissue growth. *Canine Platelet Rich Plasma (PRP)* offers a safe and natural cell therapy to relieve the pain of joint disease or injury, promote healing, and reduce recovery time using the dog's own blood.

+ Ketamine Infusion—works by disrupting the nervous system and is used in a few ways for dogs. We've used it for pain management with mixed results. A couple of dogs had greatly reduced pain for a few weeks after the drug was administered, while others showed only a slight improvement for just a day or two.

+ Microbubble Therapy—Many of our dogs arrive at Monkey's House with skin issues, the worst being *mange* or *flea dermatitis*. All of our dogs with skin aliments are treated at our house with this therapy. It's a process where bathwater is circulated through a *microbubble generator*. This therapy works great on dander, dirt, yeast, bacteria, or other allergens that can lodge on the hair follicles or clog pores. The organic matter adheres to the microbubble, which whisks it harmlessly away. We have a Thera-Clean system that works wonders on a dog's skin, reducing the time it takes to promote a healthy coat by weeks or even months. This process not only benefits skin but will also help with reducing chronic pain in arthritic dogs as well.

+ Reiki—This energy method of healing is a gentle, painless, yet powerful modality that works on animals and humans alike. Aunt Lisa is a Reiki practitioner and provides in-person, hands-on healing for the pups. It's based on channeling energy into the dog and activating the natural healing processes of the dog's own body, thus restoring physical and emotional well-being. During a Reiki healing session, many of our dogs become very relaxed, sometimes even falling asleep.

THE REFRIGERATOR IS THE NEW MEDICINE CABINET

Years before we opened Monkey's House, Michele started to learn as much as she could about dog nutrition. It's one of our tools to better care for the dogs, especially those with difficult medical conditions. Once again, it seemed that Monkey was the catalyst that really opened Michele's eyes to the pet nutrition world. At one point, we started to notice Monkey was just not himself; he was becoming reclusive and aggressive. Then one day, we found him hiding in our master bedroom closet. Michele made an appointment for him to see Dr. Judy Morgan. She was not our veterinarian; this was our first consultation with her. Michele, however, had attended a food therapy seminar taught by

Dr. Morgan and was very intrigued by her holistic approach, which includes Traditional Chinese Veterinary Medicine.

When Michele arrived home after Monkey's appointment, I asked how it went and whether Dr. Morgan had any insightful recommendations. I knew she practiced integrated veterinary medicine incorporating traditional and alternative therapies into her practice. I was anxious to hear her findings.

"Frogs' lips, turnip root, and chicken's feet is what she said to give Monkey," Michele said.

"What?" I said, startled. Then I noticed Michele laughing.

"No, but she did recommend beef heart, hardboiled eggs, and sardines," she added. Apparently, Monkey's system had "dried out" because we had changed his diet from high-moisture food to dry Kibble, which affected his mental acuity. Within a couple of days on this new food regimen, Monkey was back to his normal self. It was clear we had contributed to his condition. We had just spent a small fortune trying to save one of our horses and had switched Monkey's food to a cost-friendly variety that equated to lesser quality.

After that experience, Michele never turned back and became Dr. Morgan's greatest protégé; she continues to learn everything she can about nutrition from experts across the country. With her nursing background, she's a natural. I liken her to a sponge, soaking in as much knowledge as possible, to be the best steward she can be to hospice dogs, providing them the greatest opportunity to enjoy their life. Dr. Morgan saw this drive in Michele and was very supportive of our opening Monkey's House; she's been on our Board as the Medical Director since the beginning.

Food therapy at Monkey's House begins with a comprehensive evaluation of the dog—medical issues, blood work, allergies, and weight. From these factors, an individualized diet is designed for optimum health. The base food is generally turkey, beef, rabbit, or chicken, but we've also used llama, alpaca, venison, and moose in specific cases. We can't forget the most nourishing parts, such as heart, organ meat, and tripe. A vast array of supplements are used along with the traditional medications prescribed by the veterinarian.

Have you ever wondered how one thing in your life can be so organized, yet other aspects feel like one massive junk drawer? Case in point: The feeding routine is like clockwork right down to the food prep counter for the approximately twenty-five dogs. Distinct labels indicate a dog's bowl preference—metal, glass, paper—and bowl size. There is a list of which base meats each dog gets, another list for supplements, and last but not least, fifteen or so pill containers for each day of the week, AM and PM, just like the ones we would use. NASA would be impressed with this setup, but please don't look at our laundry room!

I think we've all heard the statement related to age: "Sixty is the new forty." When it comes to nutrition, we like to say, "The refrigerator is the new medicine cabinet." We have found food therapy to be the ace up our sleeve not only to provide the dogs with quality in their time remaining but also to provide *quantity* of time in a majority of cases. We are extremely grateful for extending these pups' lives; however, our number-one goal is always to ensure quality of life so they can enjoy those special moments.

DAISY MAE—RECONDITIONED BUT GARGANTUAN

Have you ever gotten something "reconditioned" and wondered if you did the right thing? We wondered that very thing when our Daisy Mae, a Chihuahua, made her way to us in July of 2015. She had two very large hernias, a severe heart murmur, and her eyes were always dilated so she didn't see well during the day. From sheer neglect, her toenails looked like rams' horns, and she was hairless due to malnutrition. She was also terrified of people, so much so that we had to wear falcon gloves just to handle her those first days. To be honest, I wasn't sure we could help Daisy Mae; I actually thought that maybe the best course of action would be to help her to the Rainbow Bridge. This is when we just started Monkey's House; at that time, I hadn't witnessed the "miracles" Michele would accomplish over the coming years. She assured me that we needed to give Daisy Mae a chance at life. Michele has a keen sense of knowing when to give a dog the time it needs to turn the corner and when it needs assistance to the Rainbow Bridge. Ever since Daisy Mae,

I've never questioned Michele's wisdom with the dogs again.

Daisy was "factory reconditioned" through a difficult and challenging surgery by Dr. Morgan and her staff. That was a great day for our sweet Daisy! The hernias were repaired, her bladder was tucked back inside her body, and she was spayed. Michele told me in the recovery room that Daisy looked at her belly a few times, then looked up at Michele as if she were saying, "Whose belly is that?" She recovered well and was started on microbubble therapy to clean her skin and get her hair growing. With good nutrition and treatments, her hair filled back in rather quickly.

For two years, two months, and ten days, Michele had Daisy, her little shadow, by her side. She was happiest chewing on cod skins and navigating for Michele in the car. Even on a day where there was no appointment or errands to run, Michele made time for the two of them to be in the car, no keys needed as they never left the driveway. We don't play favorites, but I think Daisy was one of Michele's. When Michele was heading up to bed, Daisy was right in her arms. Daisy was

Daisy's Halloween costume suited
her well as she was a busy bee!

always game to jump in a pile of pups, and was a champion snuggler. Before her appearance in our CNN videos featuring her snoring like a sailor, Daisy had top billing in my office party skit as Yoda. She may have had a tiny broken body, but it came with a gargantuan persona. She loved passionately and hated like a Chihuahua only can. We love a spunky hospice dog!

"SIR" COTTON

Cotton was a southern boy that came to Monkey's House all the way from the Tar Heel State, North Carolina. He was transferred to us from Hart-2-Heart Rescue; his loving foster parents Sandy and Scott drove him over eight hours from North Carolina to New Jersey so he could get the additional care he needed to live as full a life as possible. They were able to start his transformation from a dog in poor condition to teaching him to walk again, helping him gain some much-needed weight, and ridding him of fleas so this Pekinese could grow out his beautiful, white coat.

Even before Cotton arrived at Monkey's House, Michele made an appointment for him to have a thorough exam by Dr. Noelle Knight, a veterinarian at PetPT Pet Rehabilitation and Physical Medicine. We knew he was in renal failure and were very interested to find out why his gait was so slow and clumsy. Cotton had broken a pelvis at some point in his life that severely atrophied his right hind leg; he was in a fair amount of pain. Pain management was tricky due to his failing kidneys, but we needed to get him some relief. He was on a holistic diet ideal to support the kidneys, and he was started on the underwater treadmill, which was followed by cold laser therapy. For Cotton, the underwater treadmill took some weight off his injured pelvis, reducing his pain, while the steady rolling belt underwater encouraged him to use a more normal gait. The downside for Cotton: His silky white hair had to go temporarily until we got him sorted out. The upside of this therapy: Cotton was walking all the way to the end of the drive and back, 880 feet, on his daily walk.

Cotton strutting his stuff on the underwater treadmill.

Let's just say Cotton was not a fan of needles, and he would let you know it, so much so that FEMA contacted us because they were thinking of using his scream for the Emergency Broadcast System. It would surely get your attention! I guess we should have stayed away from trying acupuncture, but we've seen the benefits with many of our other dogs; we had to give it a shot. Despite medication, yummy food, and even in the safe and loving arms of his favorite veterinary technician, Savannah, Cotton decided it was not happening, no way, no how, just plain old NO! Being so distraught, acupuncture would have been counterproductive and not in his best interest. In a case like this, laser acupuncture might have been an alternative instead of using needles. He was the first of our pups to have this issue. When Michele got back from the PetPT, she told the gang that Cotton was "kicked out" for being a rabble-rouser; he took it as a badge of honor, walking into the house like a proud peacock.

The holistic diet tailored specifically to address Cotton's kidney failure worked wonders; after a few months, his blood work was excellent! Food therapy has been a powerful ally in lessening or resolving many of our dog's medical conditions. Cotton could not have been happier. He no longer needed *subcutaneous fluids* (commonly known as *sub Q fluids*); that meant no more needles! He continued his walking out to the mailbox, albeit slow and not so steady.

Cotton went on all our field trips but made his way there in the lap of one of our aunts in their car, not Waggin' One. He thought all travel should be done on four paws, not in a vehicle, and would sound that emergency alarm at the onset, eventually calming down thanks to the comfort of a loving aunt. On these occasions, Cotton became "Sir" Cotton. We had to throw in the "Sir" because he was always paired up with Princess Granny, and she could be a bit of a royal snob. They would travel in luxury in their carriage with an occasional short walk to stretch their legs. They had Aunt Karen trained well. Living life to the fullest, that's what Cotton certainly did. Michele recounted to me the following scene she had witnessed:

"Aunt Karen had everyone fed before I even got downstairs. I heard her laughing and saw Cotton upside down. Funny, touching, beautiful, over the top...I don't care what you call it, just pure love. Over a year ago, Cotton was a much different dog. He was broken by people; it only seems right that he now demands to be fed with a spoon, upside down, in-between belly rubs."

During the time Cotton spent at Monkey's House, we let him know how deeply he was loved and that he mattered.

HANNAH BEAR—"LARGE AND IN CHARGE"

Hannah Bear was one of the most stunning dogs that ever called Monkey's House home. She had beautiful, long, silky black hair with reddish-brown highlights throughout her lovely coat. This wasn't always the case for this sweet Pomeranian mix. When she joined us in October of 2017, she virtually had no hair from the neck down because of malnutrition. She looked like a Pom-corgi mix from the shoulders forward and a Chinese crested from the shoulders back. But the bigger issue was her ulcerated and cancerous mammary masses. Her huge, ruptured mass drained constantly and was so large it caused her front leg to swing out around it. She had lived a life of neglect and was abandoned in horrid condition. Like all the dogs we pull off the euthanasia list, she was on the list for what was wrong with her; no one could see all that was right with her.

Surgery was needed to remove the cancer-filled masses, but there was one problem. The masses were so large, Dr. Morgan didn't think there would be enough skin left to completely close her chest after surgery. Weeks before the surgery, an herbal paste called *neoplascene* was applied to the masses. This herbal salve selectively attacks cancer cells. While the formula was doing its job reducing the masses, we worked to improve Hannah's nutritional status and overall physical health. Her x-rays showed some fluid in the space around her lungs, which was the way her cancer spread; she was diagnosed with lung cancer. We researched the best diets to fight cancer and contacted the KetoPet Sanctuary (KetoPet). She was put on a Ketogenic diet, which may have helped slow the progression of cancer by starving cancer cells, along with supplements to support her organs and boost her immune system, as well as Chinese herbs.

Hannah Bear came here full of cancer but defied the odds, living and loving life to the fullest. She had a better quality of life than any of us could ever have imagined. Hannah was one of the sweetest and most loving dogs ever, at least toward people. Upon her arrival, she had an affinity toward cats, and not in a good way. She really loved to chase and annoy the heck out of them. Hannah abided by an old Chinese proverb, "To catch the cat, one must become the cat." Thankfully, this phase gave way to her eventually snuggling with them with an occasional chase, just to keep things fresh. Hannah was "large and in charge," picking a new cat or dog friend to stalk, hunt, and annoy on a daily basis. Big dogs, tiny dogs, slow-moving dogs, or cats—she was versatile and tenacious. Whenever I picked her up and carried her around the house, her tail never stopped wagging. She was always busy and happy; we loved her sharp attitude. Hannah loved being on the sofa with Michele. At first, we thought she just adored Michele's company, but what she really liked was being able to watch over her kingdom.

Car rides were one of her favorite pastimes, so Michele would take her to veterinary appointments even when she wasn't scheduled to be seen. That's actually one of Michele's "things," taking dogs on trips when they don't have appointments. She loves to get them out on little adventures. Our plan is to take the pups to the veterinary offices when they don't need to go, get them familiar with the setting and people that the dog, in this case Hannah, would eventually be interacting with. When they finally do have a vet appointment, the stress level will be minimized.

This plan worked out well at PetPT as Hannah got to meet Aunt Beth in action. She thought the treadmills were really cool, and after meeting Dr. Knight, decided she really liked her, too. Of course, Hannah being Hannah, she tried to cop some crackers from the purse of one of the veterinary technicians; oops. She certainly enjoyed her fun days out. However, as her lung cancer progressed, Hannah's breathing became more labored; Michele

Before Monkey's House. Hannah was in horrible condition with no hair from the neck back.

At Monkey's House. Hannah flourished and loved her adventures. (Brigantine Beach, NJ.)

was hoping acupuncture would help her breathing. While acupuncture helped her airways stay as open and healthy as possible, in the end, the procedure stressed her too much and was counterproductive.

Hannah Bear had designated herself as one of the Monkey's House spokesdogs. When we had a fund-raiser at a local restaurant, she insisted on attending and strutting her stuff. This had gone to her head a little as she always demanded to be on my lap if I were watching TV, and she also slept right in the middle of our bed. We had to be prepared; we couldn't just reach out and pet her in the middle of the night. We had to commit at least five minutes to serious belly-rub time. Let's just say we may have been sleep deprived, but Hannah was never disappointed!

We celebrated Hannah Bear's life; in those two and a half years of love and adventure, she taught us to believe in miracles. She lived a very full life with cancer, was fearless, energetic, and maybe a touch crazy, but she made every day a blast. From loving the summer trips to the beach, playing in the surf, to our winter trips in the Pines trouncing through the snow, she loved it all. She didn't let cancer get her down; if only we could all have that spirit. What a tragic loss it would have been had her story ended in a shelter, never making her way to Monkey's House that cool fall night. We were able to rewrite Hannah's story and give it a much better ending.

ADORABLE ARCHIE

When Archie first walked into Monkey's House, it was like he knew the deal. This goofy, lovable yellow Lab was a giant compared to most of our crew, so we let him meet the pups one at a time. Hannah Bear gave him an earful and had to be reminded several times that she was once a newbie. She didn't care; she just wanted him to understand she was ready to take him down any time, any place. He was a big, gentle soul who was very accepting of the crazy little dogs.

How could such an adorable guy like Archie find himself in a shelter away from his family? His owners were moving and couldn't take their twelve-year-old companion with them. The shelter found him to be terribly arthritic and thought he had bone cancer; by looking at his gait, you could see it was painful for him to get around. It didn't help that he was about thirty pounds overweight, coming in well over one hundred pounds. His ears were also misshapen from years of infections and head shaking. After suffering a seizure, the shelter felt he needed hospice placement. Luckily, he found his way here. The first line of business was to work through our laundry list of concerns. He had initial blood work and x-rays taken, and a few weeks later had a dental, neuter, and repeat x-rays in a few areas of concern, mainly his wrists and knees.

One of our concerns with Archie was his lameness and how to control his pain. We quickly put him on a tailored diet and brought his weight down about thirty pounds. Now for the biggest concern— cancer! Did he have it in that wrist? The shelter veterinarian seemed to believe he did. Thankfully, additional tests told us he didn't have cancer, which was a huge relief. Our next thought was how to improve his well-being and wrist and joint mobility. Although he loved to take walks, we limited how long they were because we didn't want to irritate the joint and cause excessive pain.

Archie was a good candidate for *platelet rich plasma* (PRP), a natural cell therapy procedure we did on his wrist and both knees. *Regenerative medicine* is very exciting and provides good results; we are so fortunate that it is one of Dr. Knight's specialties. Shortly after Archie's treatments, we saw a noticeable difference in his gait.

Hide-and-seek was one of Archie's favorite games, albeit he really wasn't that good at the hiding part. Our front porch is closed in with lattice work with a gate, so we don't have any escapees bolting from the house. It was also a good place to feed Archie during nice weather, since he was a big fan of "sharing" food that belonged to other dogs. One morning, we put him on the porch with his breakfast; a few minutes later when Michele went to get him, he was gone. She came back in the house and asked if I had already brought him in; I said no. She told me the gate had been latched. As she opened the door to go look for him, there he was, standing right there waiting to come in. Michele was puzzled but figured out his trick during breakfast the next day; when she opened the door to let him in, he was squeezing his big body through a little hole in the lattice… back onto the porch! She caught him midway through the lattice hole with a look on his face that said something like, "You're it."

Everybody loved Archie. With a happy tear in Michele's eye, she announced with great joy that Archie was an "imposter" and ready for his forever family. Why would we attach the label of "imposter" to a dog we clearly loved? If you heard somebody being called an *imposter*, you would probably avoid that person; surely you would rather be with somebody who's considered honest or genuine. However, at Monkey's House, "imposter" is one of the happiest words to hear. You'd be surprised at the joy the word brings to the aunts, uncles, and Michele and me.

An "imposter" at Monkey's House is a dog whose health has been thoroughly evaluated, and it's determined that the dog is no longer in need of hospice care. In being true to our mission, Monkey's House rescues hospice dogs diagnosed by the shelter veterinarian to be terminally ill. In most cases, we don't have the luxury of time to fully vet the validity of that determination when we pull them, sometimes just hours before the inevitable. Then, through our life-enhancing measures, we realize the dog doesn't belong here; it's not in need of hospice care. It is in need of its own forever family.

To acknowledge that one of the dogs is an imposter brings on a flood of emotions; of course, we are thrilled that the dog is not terminal and will have its own family to love it. At the same time, we have fallen in love with the dog and the dog has fallen in love with us. The emotions are much like that of fosters, maybe a little deeper, as we were part of their journey, bringing health into their lives. When Michele was on the *Hallmark Channel's Home & Family* show, the host put it quite simply, "Dogs fake that they are dying to get to Monkey's House."

We don't adopt dogs out at Monkey's House; our mission is to care for hospice dogs and we're not prepared for that function. With Archie, we partnered with Brookline Labrador Retriever Rescue to find a loving family. Aunt Karen fostered Archie to prepare him to be in a regular home setting. It didn't take too long for our precious, intoxicatingly joyful yellow Lab to find himself the most wonderful family in the world! He has doting, loving parents and a brother. Although we all shed a few tears, we are so very happy for him. Go Archie!

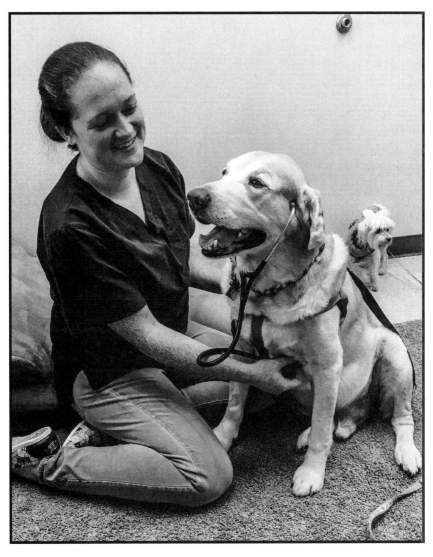

Archie agreed with Dr. Knight; he had a strong heart full of love!

CHAPTER 5

A BOY AND HIS DOG

You'll find children paired up with dogs throughout modern-day history in TV shows like *Lassie* (and *Tommy*), cartoons such as *Snoopy* (and *Charlie Brown*), and the famous Norman Rockwell *Saturday Evening Post* cover paintings depicting dogs joining in children's adventures or patiently waiting by their sides. Dogs have always been perceived as loyal companions, but they seem to be so much more to a child. The family dog is another friend to the resident kids, part of their neighborhood gang. However, to special-needs children, a dog can be their world, their very best friend, sometimes their only true friend. There is no judgment from a dog, just pure love between two kindred souls.

Kaiden is the youngest Monkey's House volunteer; he started when he was just three years old. His mom is Aunt Holly Jones who joined in our mission a few years ago in a big way. She runs a dog-walking and pet-sitting business, a one-woman show called, "Get Your Paws on Dog Walking & Pet Sitting." A mutual friend of Michele's and Holly's thankfully got them together, and the rest is history. Besides coming to help at the house a few times a week, she's been a quarantine foster for many of our dogs and is a constant forever foster, generally with three Monkey's House dogs at any given time. Her husband, Tom, is supportive of her work, and Kaiden is ecstatic at only having pups as brothers and sisters.

Autism spectrum disorder (ASD) is a neurological and developmental disorder that affects how a person acts and interacts with others, communicates, and learns. It's estimated one out of fifty children in the United States have been diagnosed with ASD. Kaiden is one of the nearly 2 percent of the entire population of children who have this disorder. He is also one of the lucky ones as research has found that dogs have an amazing impact on the quality of life and development of children with ASD. Some of the many benefits include:

+ Decreased anxiety and acts of aggression
+ Increased willingness to try new things
+ Decreased frequency of "meltdowns"
+ Increased ability to face fearful situations
+ Increased vocabulary and verbal communication
+ Increased sense of security

Kaiden has befriended many of the Monkey's House dogs, but there are three that have really stood out in my mind as being his favorites.

HARLEY, PROTECTOR AND COMPANION

To the nondog person, seeing a large Alaskan malamute mix with a little three-year-old boy draped over him while taking a nap might be frightening. To dog lovers it's a heavenly sight; we would love to be that little boy. Harley was full of love for the Jones family, her forever foster family. She especially took to Kaiden. Dog parents have endearing traits that they use to describe their fur babies: friendly, loving, high or low energy. For Kaiden, Harley was his protector and comforting companion.

Harley joined us in February of 2017. She was not an old dog like most that make their way to Monkey's House, more middle-aged. On her left hind quarter was a mass the size of a basketball, over fifteen pounds. The mass was really visible because she was so emaciated. Along with having a mass that prevented her from laying down com-

Harley and her boy Kaiden.

fortably, her hair was so matted, you couldn't get a comb through it. Eventually it became a beautiful, full coat.

The first line of business was to get Harley cleaned up and to start feeding her with some yummy, healthy food to put weight on her. It took a few months to get Harley healthy enough to undergo a lengthy and serious debulking procedure (the surgical removal of a tumor.) On her final visit to see Dr. Morgan before her surgery, Harley actually came in overweight. Dr. Morgan was shocked and asked what her diet consisted of. We informed her it was the dietary plan we had all agreed upon, but Holly mentioned that she had caught Kaiden giving Harley some pizza crust. When Holly asked Kaiden about that, he said that he only had given Harley pizza crust "once or twice." He also told her, however, that every morning he gave Harley the green Lucky Charms out of his cereal bowl. He thought it would bring her good luck for the surgery.

Even though Harley's weight was not ideal, she sailed through the surgery with flying colors. She was very fortunate to have Dr. Morgan's talented surgical mind and hands for the successful removal of that nasty "basketball," plus, of course, the magic of the Lucky Charms. After the surgery, I was able to see Harley daily for a couple of weeks. She was recovering at our house where we could keep a close eye on her while tending to her surgical incisions. Most of us take for granted simple things like laying down in comfort, something Harley couldn't experience before the surgery. She could now jump up on the sofa and lay with Kaiden, the boy she adored.

Harley underwent additional surgeries later that year to remove some mammary masses and to get her spayed. Spaying slowed down the progression of the cancer; it was determined that Harley had three kinds of cancer trying to take over her body. She was a fighter, and we made every effort to provide the tools needed to help her fight as long as she had the will. She was determined to stay strong and be with the family she adored. She was put on a Ketogenic diet, which we believed helped slow the progression of cancer by starving cancer cells. The efforts we made for Harley gave her the time to experience love and happiness. Harley was one happy pup especially when Kaiden was by her side.

Harley was the first Monkey's House dog to be in a forever foster home. The Jones family absolutely loved her, and although she wasn't crazy about car rides, she always wanted to be by Aunt Holly and Kaiden's side, so you generally saw the three together. Holly was at our house multiple times a week helping Michele with the dogs, so I got to see Harley quite often. She had her own little boy in Kaiden, but you might say she had a second one in me. I would run out to meet Harley like a kid whenever Holly pulled in the driveway. Harley always seemed to be wearing a smile that could brighten even the gloomiest day. Heaven forbid if Holly came over without Harley; that was always quite the disappointment. (No offense, Holly or Kaiden, I like to see you guys, too!)

Aunt Holly is famous for dressing up dogs for the holidays or special occasions, and Harley ate it up. Whether it was Valentine's Day or

Easter, she would be decked out to the nines and loved the attention. I especially like Holly's Halloween pictures with Harley and Kaiden in their superhero costumes.

"Miss Sassy Pants" was Holly's nickname for Harley. She was no fan of the heat and demanded her own patio umbrella to keep the sun off, a cooling vest, and her own misting fan during the summer months. On the flip side, she absolutely loved the cold weather, particularly laying out in the snow. We would find ourselves laughing when Holly told us that Harley woke her up at 3 a.m. again so she could lay on the back deck to enjoy the cool winter air. I'm not so sure Holly's husband Tom enjoyed this nightly occurrence.

Harley fought for as long as she could; she lived much longer and had a better life than predicted. She loved with every ounce of her

Harley loved laying in the snow.

being, and she showed it every single day. Harley achieved and maintained a great quality of life for as long as possible thanks to so many people. Holly, Tom, and Kaiden were her whole world. She loved them with all she had to give. Harley— "Miss Sassy Pants"—rest easy, dear friend, until we all meet again.

FLETCHER—FULL OF COURAGE, BEAUTY, AND LOVE

When Fletcher became a Monkey's House dog in late August of 2017, he was broken in every sense of the word—covered in urine, feces, fleas, dirt, and filth, unable to stand or walk, emaciated, and with cancer growing inside and outside his body. His condition told a story of a long time of neglect, maybe a lifetime of it. We knew we couldn't stop the cancer. We placed this beautiful German shepherd in the home of the Joneses, an incredibly loving foster family. Aunt Holly, Tom, and Kaiden were his people now. It took Fletcher just a few days to realize he was safe with his new family that adored him and would show him affection. For the first time in his life, he experienced what love really felt like.

There are many types of harnesses that can be used to get a dog on its feet and walking again. The medical conditions the dog has and the size and/or breed are big factors in determining the proper harness to use, and even then, it's best to try them on to see what works best. The day after Fletcher made his way to Aunt Holly's house, Michele gave me a slew of harnesses to run over and try on him. I believe Michele wanted to go herself, but when I heard we had a new German shepherd, I made the case that I should go as I would be able to lift him better. It was a weak case. If I were a lawyer, my client would be going upriver for sure. But Michele knew I really wanted to see him because I grew up with a German shepherd and loved the breed.

Fletcher was a shell of what a healthy dog should be; however, you could see the courage in his eyes and what a beautiful dog he was, a pure German shepherd with some red tones that made for pretty highlights among his black-and-tan. After trying on a few harnesses, we found one that fit his frame and protruding ribs well and provided the support he needed whenever he had to be lifted.

A few days went by, and I got the opportunity to visit Fletcher again as Holly was running low on food and I offered to do a food delivery. Like all Monkey's House dogs, Fletcher was quickly put on a food therapy program. When I arrived there, he came walking out of the house on his own with Holly following. In just a few days, the difference was incredible! He was walking around the front yard; Holly was with him step for step. He would stop, Holly would kneel down, and he would plant a big kiss right on her face. What joy that brought to all of us!

Fletcher very quickly bonded with Kaiden, who was three years old at the time. About a week after my last visit, I made up a reason to stop by to see how he was doing. Pulling into their driveway, I noticed Kaiden and Fletcher walking together with a big stick. Kaiden was holding one end and Fletcher had the other end in his mouth. If you didn't know the circumstances, you would have thought Fletcher had helped raise Kaiden like many of our dogs have done with our children. Fletcher reminded us that life doesn't have to be as complicated

What little boy and his dog don't love playing with a stick?
Fletcher and Kaiden surely did.

as we make it. Thank you, Kaiden, for accepting Fletcher's offer of friendship and love.

We didn't know Fletcher's past, nor what the future held for him when he came to Monkey's House. For example, we didn't know Fletcher:

+ would stand and then walk again.
+ loved children, specifically his boy Kaiden.
+ loved sticks, toys, and other dogs.
+ loved grilled-cheese sandwiches.
+ hated Daylight Savings Time.

What we did know is that we would fight for him to experience a life with a loving family for as long as he had the will to survive.

Fletcher left this world in the early hours of Thanksgiving Day. He quietly left his body while his family slept. The time with this great soul was too short by our standards, but we were grateful that Fletcher had those three months. It was just long enough for him to experience the kindness he'd been deprived of all his previous life before he came to Monkey's House.

BUGSY—THE "TERMINATOR"

Bugsy is the "Terminator" of dogs. He never stops, and if you need to find him at the Jones's house, just look for Kaiden; Bugsy is always within an arm's distance of him. He's like a combination of Fletcher and Harley—a great all-around dog that likes to play yet is very protective of Kaiden. Before Bugsy came to live in the Jones's household, Kaiden never slept through the night. He would wander into Holly and Tom's bedroom in the wee hours of the morning to join them in bed. This came to an abrupt end once Bugsy became part of the family because Bugsy slept with Kaiden in his bed.

The vast majority of the dogs we take in are senior dogs. Still, we are always suspicious of the "official" age given on the surrender form; the majority of time, the listed age seems higher than the dog's actual age. Maybe it makes the owners dumping their ten-year-old dog feel better if they say the dog is fourteen, thinking that's a fair age to be euthanized. Of course, it's NOT! So we take the given age with a grain of salt. Bugsy was listed as eighteen when he came to Monkey's House, which means he surpassed his twenty-third birthday. But he was so full of energy and vitality that we know he had to be younger than that.

Bugsy made his way to us from Kentucky. He's a "bug," a cross between a Boston terrier and a pug, thus the name Bugsy. Although he was only half his desirable weight, he was very active when he arrived. On his first wellness visit, Michele did ask the veterinarian about his age because we didn't think he could be that old. The veterinarian said that while Bugsy was probably not eighteen, he was still an old guy. Whatever age he actually was, after a few months he had attained his desirable weight and was just loving life on the farm.

Bugsy and Kaiden, a great superhero team.

Because Bugsy had extensive dental disease, his canine teeth—among others—were removed to get his mouth back in shape. Besides eliminating the pain from the rotten teeth, it was a little bit of a blessing that his canines were gone; see, Bugsy is a "fear biter." Bugsy assimilated well at Monkey's House except for one aspect— new aunts and uncles. After Bugsy got acquainted with a person—generally after four or five visits—he was fine. But it was stressful for him with new people coming in and out all the time. We decided to see how he would cope at Aunt Holly's house. The move worked! Bugsy was finally where he was meant to be, with no visitors on a daily basis and his very own Kaiden to play with and protect.

Kaiden suffers from sensory overload from time to time. It is one of the more common problems in individuals with autism; their senses seem to be acutely working or not working at all. When Kaiden is suffering from one of these episodes, he becomes extremely irritable and experiences discomfort, stress, and fear. You'll see him standing with his hands covering his ears to shield himself from sensory input.

When Kaiden is having an episode, Bugsy will go to his side and rest his head on his hip. Kaiden will slowly move his hand down from his ear on the side that Bugsy is leaning and gently pet his head; shortly after, his other hand comes down. Bugsy has had no training in how to comfort a child going through sensory overload. Dogs' senses are amazing; they are much more in tune with their surroundings than we give them credit for. In one way or another and on many occasions, Michele and I have seen this unique dog supersensitivity.

Kaiden was very sad at the loss of Harley and Fletcher; he still misses them both but talks about the fun times they shared together. He did ask questions when they died, but death is not an easy concept to grasp for a three- or four-year-old. Dogs add so much to our lives; we never want to see a person, let alone a child, in pain. Talking through the loss is key with a child. How beautiful it is to allow a child to experience love and loss, to grieve in a stable, loving home... and then to move forward. Kaiden is a resilient young boy who no doubt will have many more furry friends to come in the future that will enhance his life, and he will return the favor for a dog deserving of such a loving boy and family.

Laura Sylvester is the executive director of Good Dog Service Canines, an organization dedicated to helping children and families live better lives through autism-service dog companionship. Laura and her husband, Rick, started the nonprofit after exploring numerous therapies and modalities to find just the right combination to unlock and unleash the beauty living within their son, Elliot. When I told Laura about Kaiden's interactions with the Monkey's House dogs, she was not surprised at the benefits he's experienced. I asked Laura to help me understand how Orbit, Elliot's service dog, helps Elliot in his daily life. This is what she had to say:

> *"Elliot thrives when we create a bubble of positivity around him and our entire family. Meaning, we try to surround ourselves with positive, loving people who accept Elliot just the way he is. We connect him with people who have that "life is magical" mind-set, except for when we have to adventure outside of our protective bubble and encounter others of a different mind-set. We realized going out with Elliot accompanied by Orbit was like taking the bubble with us; negativity and judgment from others was quickly turned upside down. The first thing people notice is a dog, not just any dog, but Orbit, a beautiful yellow Lab being walked by a young boy. Noticing a disability was not on the front of their minds. The world became a much kinder, gentler place, and we all felt more comfortable in it. Orbit's presence dramatically transforms our lives in a world that is still learning to understand the depth of our challenges. The impact of this shift in the emotional environment cannot be overstated in our opinion."*

Now as a team, Orbit's very presence with Elliot creates noticeable changes in Elliot such as:

+ Increased Confidence and Independence: Elliot proudly takes Orbit's leash with his head held high. Before he had Orbit, he would walk timidly and withdraw into himself.
+ Increased Sociability: Elliot has more social interaction

with his peers because Orbit acts as an icebreaker in public settings and takes the focus off his disability.

* Improved Health and Physical Behavior: Elliot is less anxious and fearful, cries and becomes emotionally upset less often, shouts and screams less, and is less agitated.

Laura continued:

"Orbit is a hero to our family; his very presence reminds us to focus on what is important: love, acceptance, and the joy of being connected. He is a fun-loving companion that also knows when it's time to move into service tasks and go to work. He is not only Elliot's service dog but also sometimes pulls double duty as an ambassador for autism-assistance dogs everywhere."

CHAPTER 6

HOME FOR THE HOLIDAYS

The holidays can be a great time of joy for many and a time of sorrow for others. At Monkey's House, we've been blessed to have our sadness turn into joy. Since we started fostering ill dogs, it's been difficult to attend many holiday gatherings. After opening Monkey's House, it's been next to impossible. On occasion, we'll have a gracious aunt or uncle offer to watch the kids for a few hours while we rush off to be with our human family then rush home again. Honestly, we've come to really enjoy being with our large furry family on the holidays. It's become our comfort zone, full of unconditional love.

Like many holiday gatherings, you may create great memories and have a blast; others you may just want to forget. Thankfully, the holidays have been mostly joyful for us in many ways. Although we have pleasant memories of the holidays, it's not actually about the event but the dogs that have impacted our lives in some way around the holiday itself. When many are celebrating the holidays, Michele and I are celebrating the dogs that made their way to Monkey's House and realized they could love and be loved. People have told us that we've made such a difference in these dogs' lives; we'll be the first to tell you they've exerted a greater influence on us. Bringing joy into our lives, isn't that what holidays are really all about?

BETTY—FROM "CHAIN DOG" TO "IMPOSTER"

The first year we opened Monkey's House, Betty came via transport the day after Thanksgiving. She was pulled in the nick of time; she was about to be euthanized at ACCT, Philadelphia's only open intake shelter. ACCT is normally overcrowded because of the volume of dogs surrendered, even more so around the holidays. Unadoptable dogs like Betty are generally euthanized within a few days. She was an SPCA cruelty case and taken from her owners because of neglect and abuse. We rarely get a clear picture of a dog's past, but like Shadow, Betty was another one of our "chain dogs." When Betty arrived, she was in horrible condition. Her spirit was broken, she was severely malnourished and underweight, and she had a tumor hanging off her stomach. At the bottom of the tumor were open ulcers. We couldn't imagine the

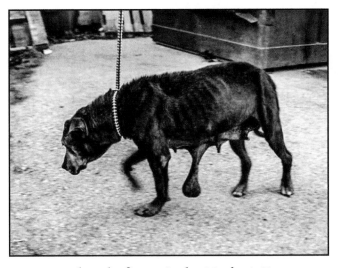

Betty when she first arrived at Monkey's House.

pain she experienced as the tumor dragged when she walked.

Since this was our first year as Monkey's House, we didn't have a foster lined up to quarantine Betty, so we did it at our house. The first few weeks Betty lived in the Cottage isolated from the other dogs. Michele jumped into action. The first thing she did was design a belly band that would hold the tumor off the ground; this stopped the ulcer from scraping the floor. Quickly, we worked up her dietary plan. We needed to get some weight on her before she had her surgery to give her a fighting chance of successfully removing the tumor.

After six weeks, Betty gained eight pounds, which made her a good candidate for surgery. We're happy to say the tumor was not cancerous; the surgery was a complete success. She was also spayed and had painful teeth removed that had been worn down to expose the roots. As time went by, Betty's spirit started to come out, and what a great one she had hidden inside her! I quickly became attached to Betty and her to me. Michele and I spend most of our time in the main house caring for the majority of the dogs that live in there with us. Getting time in the Cottage was always a challenge, but I made an effort to spend extra time in the evenings sitting with Betty. She had a buddy named Parker, a rescued pit bull. Every evening after work, I would go into the Cottage and spend time with Betty and Parker; we generally ended up doing a little

dancing. Although Betty was deaf, they both really enjoyed my dancing; you could see them getting in the groove, and Betty would start singing along with her howling.

Betty stole our hearts, and after a few months with us she had a clean bill of health. Despite the arthritis she developed from being chained her entire life, amazingly her spirit soared. At that point, Betty was labeled an imposter and ready for her forever family!

A couple of redheads, Betty and Buster enjoying each other's company.

We partnered with One Love Animal Rescue to find a loving family for Betty. She was the first imposter that we had at Monkey's House that went through such a transformation; we all fell in love with her. Michele and I drove Betty to her foster mom's house. Vicki Watkins was a regular foster mom and had a couple dogs of her own. Vicki could see the love we had for Betty and assured us she would fit right in at her home until a suitable family was found. She showed us around her home; Betty was close by my side as we navigated from room to room. Vicki pointed out the dog door that led out to a lovely fenced-in backyard. She showed us all the different dog beds Betty could choose from to make herself comfortable. We could sense the effort Vicki was making to reassure us that Betty would be well cared for and loved.

After spending some time saying our good-byes, Michele and I tried to sneak out the front door before Betty noticed; however, she caught a glimpse of us leaving. We were doing the right thing but all of our hearts were breaking!

Vicki and her partner, Fred, fell in love with Betty; next thing you know, Fred adopted her, a *foster failure*. (A *foster failure* is somebody who falls in love with the dog they are caring for and ends up adopting it.) Betty would go on daily walks to the pond with her new parents, brothers and sister. She even helped raise foster puppies for One Love Animal Rescue. With the help of so many, Betty lived a life all dogs should have.

The Marines have a saying, "Once a Marine, always a Marine." At Monkey's House, we apply that same sentiment: "Once a Monkey's House dog, always a Monkey's House dog." For any reason, we'll accept back one of our family members, temporarily or permanently. A couple years after Vicki and Fred adopted Betty, they had a trip planned but were contemplating cancelling it because of Betty's waning health. We told them to bring her to Monkey's House as we would all love to spend some time with her. That was a very special week as the aunts, Michele, and I took turns spending quality time with our Betty.

Looking back to the day we initially dropped Betty off at Vicki's house, I remember the sorrow I felt, but knowing the good life she had with Vicki and Fred reaffirmed the decision we made was the right one. Vicki kept in touch and has shared pictures of Betty surrounded by her "puppies" or dressed in her Halloween costume. Now that beats a good Thanksgiving dinner any day. We love you, Betty.

MATT—HOME AT LAST

On a cold, snowy evening in January, Michele received a phone call from Sergeant Cooper, a Burlington county SPCA humane officer. Sergeant Cooper and her partner were called by the police to a vacant residence a few towns away from Monkey's House. The police stumbled upon an animal neglect case and needed assistance removing five dogs found living in an abandoned home. There was no electricity or running water nor sign of any dog food. The place was in shambles, yet the officers noticed there was a lack of dog feces, in fact, none. This meant the dogs were eating anything to survive.

All the dogs were in bad health, but there were two that were in desperate need of emergency veterinary care. They were rushed to a veterinary hospital. One was in critical condition, and the other, Matt, needed emergency eye surgery; the end result was the removal of his right eye. The other three dogs were taken to the shelter to recover. Unfortunately, the dog in critical condition eventually passed.

Sergeant Cooper's call was to ask Michele to foster Matt back to health while they built a case against the owner. The next day Matt arrived; he was a golden retriever that looked like he had been through the ringer. Even though he had received a bath at the veterinary hospital, he was filthy, severely underweight, and couldn't walk. Matt's horrible journey brought him to Monkey's House where the care is opposite of the horrible conditions he had lived in. To start, he received love and compassion, which all the pups receive here. Next we removed his matted hair and gave him a nice, soaking bath to get his coat clean of caked-on dirt and grime. I don't know if Matt knew it yet, but he was now part of the Monkey's House family. Ready to get spoiled?

After living without food for what appeared quite some time, Matt was thirty pounds underweight and needed a meal plan designed just for him. We fed him multiple small meals throughout the day as he needed to gain his weight back, but we wanted it to be healthy weight. His meal was made up of cooked turkey, which included various vegetables, along with probiotics and other supplements. Matt had one other major health issue; besides his eye needing to be removed and being starved, he couldn't walk on his own. His body was getting nutrients from anywhere it could, including his own muscles. A "Help 'Em Up Harness" was purchased that allowed us to gently lift him. In this way, with the harness supporting most of his weight, he was able to walk. This went on for a few weeks until he was strong enough to walk on his own.

Matt loved being a farm dog.

Matt had physical therapy, in particular the underwater treadmill that helped him walk with the aid of the buoyancy from the water. Over time Matt was walking again, playing with his tennis ball, and eating marrow bones that he especially loved. Within a couple of months, he gained back those needed thirty pounds; once again, he was a proud, handsome golden retriever. He really started to enjoy his new life as a farm dog, and boy did he look the part walking with Michele, me, or the many aunts and uncles around the property. Probably for the first time in his life, he was truly a happy dog and got to experience real love.

All along, the SPCA humane police were building a case against the owner. The owner was inquiring about Matt and wanted to see him. We wanted nothing to do with her, nor did we want her around Matt. Michele's "momma grizzly" came out and we would not let her come to Monkey's House. However, as most of us know, laws are generally not in support of the dogs; most states consider a dog as property. We were ordered to allow the owner to see Matt. Michele unwillingly drove Matt to a neutral location where Sergeant Cooper oversaw the visit. Matt wanted nothing to do with his so-called owner. The entire experience was very upsetting to Matt, Michele, and me.

Matt loved his life at Monkey's House as he made many friends big and small, even befriending our resident cat at the time, Sammy. As everything seemed to be falling into place, we noticed a few changes in Matt and took him to see Dr. Morgan. Sadly, Matt was diagnosed with bone cancer in late April; it became very painful for him. When we thought it was time for him to go to the Rainbow Bridge, the "owner" would not consent. We had to go through other channels to release Matt's soul from his broken body. This took time, time Matt did not have as he was in agony, and we were in hell.

We fought for Matt and won. Finally, we got the approval to assist Matt so he could meet our crew at the Bridge. He was surrounded by many that loved him, humans and dogs, wrapped in a prayer blanket as he gently made his way to heaven.

The end—not quite. The nightmare with this "owner" continued; she wanted Matt's body back. ALL Monkey's House dogs live here forever; we know their spirits go to the Rainbow Bridge, but their bodies stay on the farm. It was heartbreaking, and it felt like we let Matt down again by giving up his body.

The day before Thanksgiving, roughly six months after Matt's passing, Sergeant Cooper notified us that after a long court battle the owner reclaimed her living dogs but left Matt behind in the shelter's freezer.

I quickly called the shelter and told them I was coming for Matt. I grabbed my wallet and keys as fast as I could, hopped in my car, and raced to the shelter. When I got there, Matt was waiting for me. I gently put him on my backseat and headed home. As I drove down our country road, I felt a huge weight lifted off of my heart. When I reached our little farm, I was overrun with emotions as tears ran down my face. Michele and I couldn't have asked for a better Thanksgiving. Matt came home that day.

CHAPTER 7

LOVE AT FIRST WIGGLE

Michele appeared on the *Hallmark Channel's Home & Family* TV show to introduce the audience to Monkey's House, explaining our mission. One of the questions the cohost Debbie Matenopoulos asked Michele was, "Is it sad for you when a dog passes?"

"It rips out a piece of my heart each and every time; the day I don't feel that is the day I stop. They deserve all of my heart," Michele answered. I couldn't agree more with Michele and I'd like to add that it doesn't matter if that dog was here days, weeks, months, or years. We have the same emotions when they pass.

Some people equate the length of time a dog lived with us with the depth of sorrow we should feel when it passes. It's very sad to lose any one of our furry family members no matter how short or long the time we had with them. I understand the bond grows over time, but having less time with a particular dog doesn't mean we feel less sorrow upon losing that dog. What Michele and I find the hardest to understand are the folks who think just because Michele and I run a dog hospice day and night that death shouldn't affect us as much as it does the "normal" pet parent. If a dog has only been here a short period of time—I get the sense from some folks—then we shouldn't be heartbroken. Actually, for what we do I think it's even sadder. We didn't have the time to show them what love really looked and felt like. We didn't get to show them that not all people are bad, that they could put their trust in us, snuggle in our arms, and make a few new furry friends. We didn't get the time to show them how to enjoy life maybe for the first time in their lives.

For every dog that comes into Monkey's House, it's "Love at First Wiggle" for us.

BO— "THIEF OF HEARTS"

We received a call from one of our local shelters just after we opened in 2015. They had a young yellow Lab mix that needed a miracle. This handsome boy named Bo was suffering from severe *hip dysphasia* and *megaesophagus*. *Megaesophagus*, also known as *ME*, is a condition in which the esophagus is enlarged and the dog can't get or keep food down in the stomach. Bo required small frequent feedings while being kept perpendicular to the ground. This position encouraged food to fall into his stomach by gravity.

Because of ME, Bo was very small for a Lab and had a frail body. However, what he lacked in stature he made up for in his will to live and love. He had an extraordinary disposition; he was a sweetheart and was given the nickname, "Thief of Hearts." In running Monkey's House for five years now, it's amazing to see that dogs like Bo, the

With Bo, it was love at first glance

sickest of the sick, are the ones with the most loving personalities. As Michele often says,

"Hospice dogs can teach us so much. If only humans could learn to relish their final days like these wonderful souls."

Once Bo made his way to Monkey's House, we quickly needed to learn as much about ME as possible to give him the support he needed. Michele reached out to an ME support group, Upright Canine Brigade, to gather as much knowledge as she could. A *Bailey chair* was ordered; this special chair positions the dog in an upright, seated position to help food navigate down into the stomach. In the meantime, one of us would sit with Bo as he ate. As we waited for the chair to arrive, Michele came up with a great idea. (Sometimes you have to think outside of the box.) We took a clean garbage can, lined it with a comforter, and we slid Bo gently into it so he was in an upright position. One of us would sit with him as he ate; we'd be there for thirty or forty minutes, thinking the food went down and stayed down. Unfortunately, it was only positive thinking, because just minutes after we thought he had success, he would regurgitate it. This process was carried out three or four times a day to get needed nutrients into Bo's weakened body.

Bo was such a good patient; his spirits ran high with his tail constantly wagging even when his body was failing him. He received his medications and fluids to stay hydrated, nebulizer treatments (a nebulizer changes liquid medicine into an aerosol mist that are then inhaled through a mask. It was used to deliver bronchodilator medication to open his airway), chest physiotherapy (brisk percussion of the chest wall helps to break up and dislodge mucus), to assist his cough, and hourly short walks to keep his lungs and bowels working. We had hoped that he would have time to enjoy life before he went to the Rainbow Bridge. Regardless, he was warm, he was not alone, and he knew he was loved.

His entire time at Monkey's House, his tail would wag with his eyes wide and bright. He wanted to be with us till the end. On his last day, I remember coming home from work, driving up the driveway, and seeing Michele taking Bo out for a short walk in front of the Cottage. Even from a distance, I could tell his body was done; he just looked so tired. As I started to walk over to greet them, Bo noticed it was me. As I got closer, his tail started to wag ever so slightly, and his eyes widened, which said to me, "Love you, Dad; thanks for caring for me."

Bo, we loved you, and not for just nine days; you'll be loved forever in our hearts.

CASEY—A TRUE SWEETHEART AND A GENTLE SOUL

You've probably all experienced the feeling of "being in the right place at the right time" at some point in your lives. Thankfully, for a sweet dog named Casey, this was the case. Casey had a little poodle named FiFi to thank for her adoption into Monkey's House. FiFi had just joined our crew but needed to be rushed to Dr. Morgan's office because she was in diabetic shock. Thankfully, FiFi was stabilized and Michele made her comfortable for the car ride home.

Just as Michele left the office, a good samaritan brought Casey into Dr. Morgan's office for euthanasia. Casey's owner had died, leaving the neighborhood to intermittently care for her. Things were taking a turn for the worst for Casey, and the folks in the community were no longer able to care for her. She was carrying a thirty-five-pound mass on her back. She was a mixed breed with what looked like a little shepherd in her. Dr. Morgan thought she was a candidate for Monkey's House and quickly called Michele. At this point, Michele was only fifteen minutes into her trip home so she quickly made a U turn and went back to Dr. Morgan's office to meet Casey. Michele readily accepted the new challenge of caring for this sweet girl who had ended up in a bad situation through no fault of her own.

When she first arrived at Monkey's House, Casey seemed strong; her physical exam and blood work were reasonably good, and we had hoped to give her a second shot at life. Believe it or not, her broken heart over her deceased owner was her greatest burden.

Within just a couple of days, Casey made great progress. She was no longer scared of her surroundings; she was a bit more willing to have her picture taken. Her tail wagged when she saw us, when we fed her, and when we talked to her. She was a true sweetheart. The mass didn't appear to be causing her pain, at least from what we could tell. The biggest issue we noticed was her difficulty in balancing herself when she walked because of the sheer size of the tumor. Michele designed a sling to support her when she walked; we were always by her side to assist her with her balance. We loved watching her come out of her shell. After the initial shock of seeing the mass, it became easy to look past it and just fall in love with her. We certainly did.

Casey. The love through her eyes
had the ability to hypnotize.

Casey weighed in at seventy pounds. After subtracting the thirty-five-pound mass, that meant she was a thirty-five-pound dog, which was extremely underweight for her frame. The game plan was to get some weight on her before she had surgery. It's optimal for a dog to be near normal weight when going through an extensive procedure. Her blood work was great. We just needed some time to build up her strength and get weight on her. As Casey waited, she was showered with love.

As you know, the best-laid plans don't always work out. Casey was getting weaker, and although she was with us just a couple of weeks, the tumor seemed to be taking in all the nourishment we were hoping would strengthen her. The tumor, not her body, was growing. The time for action was at hand; the risks were huge, but we were out of options and couldn't wait any longer. Something had to be done immediately.

As Michele said,

"We were hoping we could help her, but honestly, we just didn't know at that point. The plan was to try to remove the mass. The shot for euthanasia and the shot for anesthesia are basically the same. We had nothing to lose by trying, and Casey had everything to gain. As she settled in at Monkey's House, Casey appeared tired. The odds were not in her favor, but we wanted her to have a life and feel loved for whatever time she had. I put out a request to our aunts and uncles asking them, if they were up to it, to come spend one-on-one time with Casey. The response was incredible. All I can say is that our team had me in tears, inspired by their strength and love. Casey's dance card filled quickly and she was loved fiercely.

At the surgery, I looked into her eyes as she fell asleep and promised her she would either wake up minus a huge burden and be able to enjoy a much easier life or (be with) her owner who was deceased and who she seemed to miss very much. Her heart stopped a few times during her surgery. I whispered in her ear to please fight. She did, but each time her heart stopped, the risk of harsh postoperative complications increased. The miracle of life was not to be had that day. The mass was removed and her perfect, little body was neatly sutured up. As my heart broke, I could almost feel a sense of her running, something she probably hadn't done for a very long time. I brought her home that day; our farm was where she belonged. It was an honor for all of us at Monkey's House to know and love her and we're eternally grateful to everyone who helped us give her love and a shot at life."

I'll never forget the last evening I spent with Casey, laying on the floor next to her. She was such a gentle soul. Our time with Casey lasted only a few weeks, but our memories and love for her will last a lifetime.

PETE AND A DOG'S PURPOSE

One of the more common bumper stickers or magnets related to dog rescue that you'll see on the back of a car is, "WHO RESCUED WHOM?" I think it's safe to say that most dog parents will tell you that they feel they are the ones who have been rescued by their beloved companion. At Monkey's House, you might think it's a little different as most of our dogs were on the clock waiting to be euthanized when we stepped in. However, Michele and I agree all of the dogs that come through our doors actually rescued us in one way or another.

In the spring of 2016, we welcomed Pete, an Australian shepherd that in his previous life was a search and rescue dog. How a dog that once saved lives ended up in a shelter ready to be destroyed is beyond me. But after the series of events that I'm about to tell you, I believe it was meant to be. Pete had a reason to end up in a shelter and then to make his way to Monkey's House.

When you run a sanctuary out of your house, vacations are very hard to come by. Finding a dog sitter for this number of dogs is not an easy task. I generally took staycations, where I worked on the farm to finish projects that got backed up because of a lack of time. I had time-off planned for the middle of March. The project I had slated was repairing a few old sheds. I purchased all the supplies ahead of time so I could hit the ground running. As that date approached, an urgent request came down from leadership at my day job, as a human resources manager at a pharmaceutical company. One thing led to another, and my vacation was postponed by two weeks. That was fine; I was only working around the farm. I didn't need to reschedule any travel plans, so two weeks later it was.

Two weeks later, Michele received a call from a local shelter the day before my staycation was finally going to start, asking us to take Pete.

We had the room, so Pete made his way to our house. The shelter veterinarian said Pete had cancer, and he also had very bad infections in his ears. When I got home that evening, Pete was already at the house. There seemed to be an instant connection between the two of us. In spite of some health issues, he was an active dog about ten years old.

As with any new dog, Pete needed to be in isolation for a couple of weeks in the Cottage to ensure he didn't have any illnesses like kennel cough. We made sure we gave him extra attention, which included a lot of walks. He was up for them and really liked getting out to enjoy the fresh air and sunshine. Our six-acre farm lot is narrow yet runs deep. Most of our walks are in our back field; you'll see the aunts and

Pete arriving at Monkey's House.

uncles, Michele or me, leading the pups around the perimeter of the field on any given day. Besides being a little bit of paradise, the field is far from neighbors as well as road traffic, although there usually is very little traffic on our back-country road.

On the Saturday just a day after his arrival, the walks began. I would take Pete out twice a day for a mile-plus-long hike. One day, I was a little more adventurous and opted to take the road with Pete, not sure why at the time, but something was leading me to stay on the road. The weather was ideal for walking. In the morning, Pete and I would get out early. I'd wear a midweight jacket as it was still fairly cool from the night before. We would walk a little over a half mile to the end of our road, turn around, and then head back. It's a scenic walk with mostly fields and woods; we only pass three houses. There was a lot of activity with the farmers preparing their fields and spring birds flitting by as the sun was starting to warm up the day. Pete was very interested in his surroundings, taking in stride all the activity. He was very comfortable on leash, an easy dog to walk.

Pete and I were really becoming buddies. I put off some of my projects to spend extra time with him. One Tuesday morning I grabbed the leash, snapped it on Pete, and off we went. As we passed the first old farmhouse, I noticed the door on the pickup truck parked in the drive was ajar. It looked like the older gentleman, Bill, was getting ready to head into town. We continued on our walk to the end of the road, turned, and proceeded to make our way toward home. As we approached the old farmhouse again, I noticed the door of the truck was still open. Pete and I walked a little closer, and we saw Bill on the ground next to the truck. We rushed over to lend assistance; he was dazed and apparently had fallen the evening before. He spent the night on the cold stone driveway with no jacket. I quickly called 911. Although Bill spent some time in the hospital, he did make a recovery and was out of the hospital in about six days. The doctors said if he had been on the ground much longer he might not have been that lucky.

A little over a week after rescuing our neighbor, Pete suddenly passed. I was heartbroken. I had grown very close to Pete and so enjoyed our time together. In analyzing the events that led up to Bill's rescue, I believe there were higher forces at work—the changing of my vacation plans; Pete making his way to us; walking on the road instead of the field. There were just too many pieces of the puzzle that came together for it to be a coincidence. I believe God has a purpose for us all, even dogs. Pete was brought to Monkey's House to save another life, his "one last save." Once accomplished, he made his way to the Rainbow Bridge. My faith in knowing that Pete fulfilled his purpose eased my pain of losing him. We'll meet again at the Bridge, Pete.

"Every dog has a purpose in life. Some find out early on, others later in their journeys, but every dog deserves the chance to find that purpose and thrive in fulfilling it. The Search Dog Foundation has committed to turning shelter dogs into search dogs who may someday rescue someone—and in the process saving lives, both human and canine. And even if he or she does not complete our training, every rescued dog that enters our program will never need to be rescued again. Thank you to Monkey's House and all the rescues and organizations doing fantastic work across the country to help each dog find its purpose in life."

—National Disaster Search Dog Foundation.

CHAPTER 8

EVERYBODY'S A COMEDIAN, EVEN HOSPICE DOGS

Aunt Tracey once said, "Monkey's House is the happiest place on earth." We couldn't agree more. Of course, we do have our sad times, but 95 percent of the time it's a joyful place. Surrounded by so many dogs, the variety of personalities is sure to put a smile on the grumpiest face, and not just on those people at Monkey's House but also on those who follow the pups on social media. Michele read me a comment one evening from one of our global family members. It said:

"I came home from work today in a bad mood, a little on the grumpy side. I guess to save himself, my husband quickly told me to go check out the Monkey's House post. It always puts a smile on my face and uplifts my spirit. Like always, tonight's post didn't disappoint; it completely changed my frame of mind."

This is not a one-off occurrence. We all know dogs are special and being with or hearing about the escapades of the Monkey's House pack is magical.

The big craze now is binge watching a series on Netflix or on one of the other streaming services. If you're like us, a multidog family, I will tell you what's more enjoyable—binge watching your pups. Watch how they interact with one another or even with you. Notice how they treat that little stuffed animal like their baby, or just listen to their different snoring sounds. Now, when you have as many dogs as we do, you're sure to find a few comedians in the mix. Their routines and style may vary, but watch out; they may just have YOU rolling on the floor this time! Stop surfing the TV channels, turn off your smartphones, squeeze into a comfy chair, and get ready to chuckle through a few of the real characters of Monkey's House.

HOOCH, THE "WILD CHILD"

Every family has a "wild child." It may be one of your children, a grand-child, or maybe a cousin, niece or nephew. Monkey's House always has a couple at any given time, but the top prize goes to Hooch, a handsome chocolate cocker spaniel. It makes sense as he was roaming the streets of Philadelphia, eluding the humane police for six weeks as they tried everything to catch him. We can only imagine Hooch laughing as he taunted them. I could see him sticking his head around the corner, giving a big bark saying, "I'm over here," and then be off and running with the dog catchers in chase, like an old Charlie Chaplin movie.

When Hooch was eventually caught, his captors realized that his left rear foot was bloodied. The rescue organization where he landed couldn't get the bleeding to stop. At that point, their veterinarian said Hooch would need a bandage on that foot the rest of his life and recommended euthanasia. That's when the rescue reached out to Michele to see if we could take Hooch. Initially, Michele had to turn them down as we were full—actually, over capacity—and he would not have been a good candidate for a forever foster. But they persisted, so we arranged to make Hooch a part of the family.

Our first priority was to see what was up with that foot of his. Michele cleaned and rebandaged it and quickly took him to see Dr. Morgan. The diagnosis was cancer, so Hooch had one toe and part of a bone in his foot removed. The surgery might have slowed Hooch down to the speed of a normal dog, but as it healed, he became full of mischief again. He returned to his Philly street dog attitude, getting into everything and anything. He would have been the perfect dog for kids, the perfect excuse when they didn't get their homework done.

Just put the papers on the edge of the table, Hooch would find them, and then the next thing you're telling the teacher is, "The dog ate my homework." And in this case, it would've been true!

After a few months at Monkey's House, Hooch developed *vestibular syndrome*, commonly known as *drunk dog syndrome*. Luckily for us, this was not our first experience with vestibular syndrome. There are many potential causes and it usually affects older dogs, and 98 percent of Monkey's House dogs are seniors.

The common term, *drunk dog syndrome*, is spot on as a dog loses its equilibrium. Hooch's loss of balance gave him a wavering gait. Along with this symptom came the famous one-sided head tilt. With his equilibrium out of balance, Hooch's brain needed time to readjust to the new situation. This took Hooch a good couple of months, yet he liked the head tilt look and decided to keep it. He thought the look would add to his comedy act and get him more treats. It worked for him.

Don't for a minute think that vestibular syndrome slowed Hooch down, nor did his second bout with cancer. Yes, the cancer came back and a second toe was removed. The cancer had also spread throughout his body, but like the other dogs at Monkey's House, he didn't dwell on it and kept living and enjoying being in the moment every day.

Hooch had a couple of favorite things he loved to do: surfing and eating bananas. You could probably say they are linked together. His love for bananas came from a successful counter-surfing mission right into Aunt Sandie's pocketbook, scoring him a nice ripe banana. He thoroughly enjoyed that banana, including the peel, stem, and sticker. He got very good at surfing for bananas. To Hooch's surprise, bananas suddenly started to fall from the sky right in front of him. Hooch even found a banana half buried in the sand at the beach, barking excitingly as if to say, "Hey, Dad, a sand-banana!" Hooch would constantly make us laugh with his shenanigans.

One of Hooch's favorite field trips was going to the Jersey Shore. On a spring trip the weekend before Memorial Day, Hooch had a blast walking on the beach and taking a dip in the ocean. Like many of us, he loved walking down the beach in about three inches of water, enjoying the sights and smells. Hooch became my inspiration for the summer of 2019 Monkey's House T-shirt. It highlights Hooch on a banana surfboard with our slogan, "Where Dogs Go to LIVE!" The shirt design is a true depiction of Hooch's attitude, carefree and happy-go-lucky. Hooch and the other dogs at Monkey's House are all living examples of one of Michele's famous quotes, "Just because you're dying doesn't mean you can't live."

Hooch at his favorite place, the Jersey Shore.

Hooch eventually did make his way to the Rainbow Bridge. I can only imagine him surfing on his banana surfboard. I just hope they have extra surfboards in heaven. Hang-10, Hooch; we love you, Dude.

CRAZY EVE

On a daily basis, Eve brings on her comedy act, what we like to call the "Bat-Crap Crazy" hour. A little silky terrier, she made her way to Monkey's House in the spring of 2017. We never know how much we can help a dog when we pull it from a shelter. We promised Eve she would never feel as bad as she felt in the shelter, that she would be loved far beyond the stars, forever. She had uncontrolled diabetes, she was blind, her kidney and liver values were elevated, and she was emaciated. We regulated her blood sugar; she received insulin twice a day. Her kidney and liver values became normal with supportive supplements that were added to her diet. She gained some weight on her tiny frame, and she had a dental procedure that left her with four teeth. Now she's always filled with joy; she's hard core, committed with her whole heart, and did we mention crazy?

One morning, Michele woke up and heard somebody growling. Worried that a fight was imminent, she quickly discovered where it was coming from. Eve was full-out attacking our poor, innocent, un-suspecting, helpless...vacuum cleaner! It's a big upright model. It was able to stand its ground until Michele could stop laughing and pull Eve away from it. We love Eve's spunk but don't get in her way. To sum up Eve: "She doesn't go crazy, she is crazy. She just goes normal from time to time!"

From what I understand, comedians are sometimes envious of one another, and Eve was not a fan of Hooch's act. She considered him a "prop comedian," using his banana and surfboard, where she uses her wit, more improv. I wonder if she thought the vacuum cleaner was Hooch at the mic?

Have you ever had a dog that was just too smart? Eve is one of those dogs. I equate her to a rebellious teenager; at times you want to pull your hair out, yet that is who can solve your smartphone or tablet problems. Since Eve is part of Michele's entourage, she's always by Michele's side. In the evening, Michele will sit on the couch with a few pups piled up there with her, Eve included. This is when Michele does the Monkey's House social media post or her online shopping.

You never sit for long at Monkey's House; there is way too much to do or somebody needs assistance. Whenever Michele got up and left her iPad behind, it was an invitation to our little innocent Eve to play her pranks. Not once, but twice Michele's settings on her iPad were changed, first to Portuguese, then to what I believe was Korean. Eve must have gotten a good chuckle seeing me struggle to get Michele's iPad back to English.

Aunt Sandie from DI-Oh-Geez Grooming has become a "cuteness fairy" for Monkey's House. She is Eve's personal groomer. Generally after a makeover, Eve looks for trouble in all the wrong places. She's counting on the fact that her good looks will keep her out of trouble. She's probably right.

Note to all the multiple-dog families out there: When choosing a movie, stay away from dog themes. One night we decided to watch a movie, a rarity for us. We chose *Megan Leavy and Max*. It was advertised as a real-life drama based on a military bomb-sniffing dog and handler. In reality, it was an interactive singalong and led to much discussion among the pups. Have you ever noticed that people

Crazy Eve contemplating her next prank!

who are hard of hearing talk a bit louder? It's the same for deaf dogs; they bark louder. Eve seemed to be the instigator to no surprise. Every time a dog barked on TV, the ruckus—I mean cheers—would start with her. We watched a movie but didn't hear that much of it. The pups got lots of snuggles and are under the impression that they were in the movie, too. We surely aren't going to be watching any horror movies with Eve!

At the end of 2018, I created the first-ever Monkey's House calendar. It included all the dogs since Monkey House's inception. To be honest, I was elated with how nice the calendar came out. Shortly afterward, I received an e-mail from an organization called Dogs Rock International stating that Monkey's House was awarded the Gold Dog Bone in the Rescue Dog Calendar category. Michele and I were very excited to win this honor until we noticed quite a few typos along with a lot of references about giving the pups extra treats for being such good models for the calendar.

As we looked around the room to share this good news with the dogs, we noticed a few of the craftier pups were missing—as well as Michele's iPad. As Michele went looking for her iPad, to her surprise three cohorts, Eve, Hannah, and Hooch, were rolling around the floor in hysterics. You guessed it; Eve once again got ahold of Michele's password and she went to town with it. We couldn't help but laugh as they pulled a good one over on us. I can't be too hard on them; they did say we had the best calendar.

Since Eve has been here, we've had to make adjustments to the amount of insulin she receives, luckily decreasing it because of her healthy diet. At one point, however, she mysteriously became resistant to her insulin and her blood sugar shot through the roof. She was critically ill, and we were sticking her multiple times a day to check her blood-sugar level and to give her sub Q fluids. Michele went into overdrive to try to figure out what the problem was. At one point, Eve was getting Brussels sprouts and other vegetables with her meals. We ended up changing the type of insulin we gave her. Michele told me,

"People at times get overwhelmed at making big changes when their pet becomes ill or develops a chronic illness. Change is hard. We don't know if Eve ever ate veggies before. She is now great about needles but initially she didn't love the concept. It's all in how you sell it. She's happy, she knows she is loved and adored. She is healthy enough to support her special kind of crazy, her 'comedy act.' We make changes like this all the time. These dogs are old, they adjust, they figure it out, and they are happy. If you are struggling with your pet's chronic illness, reach out, work it out. It's not the end, it's just a different present."

Eve loves her life here and thoroughly enjoys all the field trips and any type of adventure. One of her favorite places is the Jersey Shore. She loves walking in the water and all the exotic ocean smells; well, they are exotic for a landlocked dog, that is. Be on the lookout for Eve's next act; you know it's going to be clever!

BULLWINKLE AND HIS COMEDY ANTICS

Bullwinkle was a one-of-a-kind treeing walker coonhound with a little bit of regular coonhound mixed in. His name fit him to a tee. He was just like the moose in the *Rocky and Bullwinkle* cartoon I used to watch growing up, awkwardly lanky in such a loveable way. This adorable hound was covered in hearts, three black-and-brown heart-shaped markings against his white coat. Sadly, for all of his hearts, he didn't seem to know much about love, treats, or affection when he came to Monkey's House. Bullwinkle was transferred here in December of 2016 from York County SPCA in Pennsylvania. What lovely people to work with; they were diligent and meticulous in answering all of our questions and in discussing if hospice care in a home setting was best for Bullwinkle.

For a comedian's stage name, Bullwinkle worked great, but around Monkey's House he was known as plain old Bull. Of course, there was nothing plain about him. He might have been the sweetest hound dog in the world; everybody who met him fell in love with him, even those who only got to know him virtually.

We estimated Bull was ten years old when he came to Monkey's House, and he had a variety of ailments. For starters, he had a horrible case of kennel cough that Peg, our quarantine foster, worked through for us. Bull had a grade-three heart murmur, spondylosis and arthritis of his spine, was an anal granuloma cancer survivor, and had many broken and infected teeth. He was deaf and nearly blind. Weighing in at eighty-five pounds, we quickly got him to his ideal weight of eighty. This was an easy task with proper nutrition. The itchy skin was resolved with bathing; we use kin+kind shampoo. Their products are natural and organic, gentle on our dogs' skin, and in line with our philosophy of avoiding harsh medicated or chemical treatments. We agree with kin+kind; nature works better. As for his stinky ears, that was resolved with due diligence; we stayed on top of the daily cleanings.

After his quarantine, Bull fit right in at Monkey's House. He loved the other dogs, cats, aunts and uncles. You name it and he loved it, especially food. Well, there was one thing he didn't love—extreme temperatures. I remember on some of the coldest, snowiest days Bull hated to go outside for potty. We would entice him to make some yellow snow; the last thing we wanted was to clean up Lake Bullwinkle. He was a two-roll paper towel guy; to this day he holds the record. I think he would be proud of that accomplishment! He didn't like the steamy hot days, either. In fact, he had his own little floor fan pointing right on him during the summer months. When needed, he would lay on a cooling mat.

It is always nice when a dog can be off-leash. With the number of dogs we have, it takes quite a while for potty breaks. Bull would go out and walk along with the leashed pups. Usually, he would peel off and hang around the front of the house. One day, Michele got into a bit of a pickle. Let your imagination go wild; Michele certainly did with her morning attire! She was sporting a pink floral nightgown under a navy-blue plaid flannel shirt, bright blue sneakers...and let's just say her hair had yet to be disturbed by a brush. With about ten dogs in tow and Bull free-ranging, Michele pulled the door shut—and it locked! Michele claims the door locks itself from time to time; who am I to doubt her? She panicked and couldn't remember the code for our emergency key box. Wouldn't you know the rest of the house was locked up like Ft. Knox? It took some thinking and creativity, but thirty minutes later, she had the ten pups back in the house. But wait, there was one missing. Where was Bull? Michele ran out looking for him, calling his name. We know Bull is deaf, but that never stops us from calling or talking to our dogs. Michele heard the chickens making a fuss and went to investigate. Bull had found his way into the chicken coop! No hens were harmed; Bull was more interested in their food! His antics always made our hearts smile.

Bull eventually got vestibular syndrome, "drunk dog syndrome." That's how we were able to handle Hooch so well; we had learned about it from Bull. He, too had a bit of a head tilt, but the bigger issue was his balance. For an eighty-pound dog that already had a weakened hind end, and as I earlier put it, was "awkwardly lanky," vestibular syndrome hit him hard. Initially he was nauseated; however, the dizziness lasted months. We put a Ruffwear harness on Bull as it gave us the ability to get him upright and assist him in getting around. He never fully gained back all his balance. Let me put it this way: He wouldn't be doing the balance-beam routine even with a two-foot-wide beam! But it all became part of his charm.

Luckily, this syndrome didn't put a cramp on Bull's comedy gig. He made us laugh on a daily basis. His routine was distorting his large body into the smallest of beds, the ones reserved for the "smalls." Now he never fully got into the bed. As he was sleeping, limbs would be hanging out everywhere. At times he would be upside down, twisted like a pretzel. He would give us a good laugh. We would gently wake him and get him over to his big bed. Many times that bed was being occupied by one of the smalls who at the time was living large!

Bullwinkle performing his comedy act of squeezing into a small bed.

The multitude of serious health problems that Bull had before coming to Monkey's House had taken turns attacking his body, his mobility, his breathing, and his dignity. Unless you knew about all his aliments, you would have no idea the physical challenges this pup endured every single day. Despite all of them, he was happy, loving, gentle, and patient. He made friends with all our dogs, big and small, and had a calm presence. He was patient when Ziggy's cart got hung up on his gigantic feet. (Ziggy was a Maltese with a paralyzed hind end who used a cart to get around.) Bull didn't always have an easy life, nor had he always been loved and adored. On top of all that was wrong with him, he had been debarked. Someone had cut his vocal cords. They took his voice and eventually tossed him aside. Yet in his sickest, most physically broken state, he gave the human race a second chance. He was willing to love the Monkey's House family.

As his body became weaker, our love for him became greater. That's when Bull realized that Arby's delivers! "Who knew that Aunt Trudy,

Aunt Terry, and Aunt Sandi all worked at Arby's," Bull probably thought. Aunt Holly promised Bull a big surprise was in the works. Boy, did she ever deliver! A gigantic plate of steak and eggs appeared for his breakfast one morning. It smelled delish! Bull ate breakfast in the sunshine on our front porch. He's so kind he even shared a few bites with Grandpa the cat. Steak and eggs are every dog's fantasy!

Keeping a dog engaged and its mind occupied is very important, especially for a dog with limited mobility. We came up with a game just for Bull called it, "find the treat in the dirty laundry pile." He thoroughly enjoyed his days of hunting for treats. He also helped Michele and the aunts clean the garage. His job was to eat the dehydrated mushrooms that seemed to be growing on the cement, then get rid of those dried cod skins that were multiplying by the minute, and one last thing, what were those dried beef lungs doing in the dog laundry pile? Bull really enjoyed those simple adventures.

Before Bull left this world, he ate three breakfasts with NO vegetables, plus two bacon sandwiches. We told the aunts to bring lots of contraband and they didn't disappoint. Laying on his big bed with his good friend LA, surrounded by his many aunts, Michele and me, Bullwinkle was assisted to the Rainbow Bridge. He joined us for eighteen months; the only things that worked well were his nose, his tummy, and his ability to love everyone and everything with his whole heart. Bull had fun, lots of it. He had adventures, friends, free will, and was loved collectively by more people then we will ever be able to comprehend.

Big brother Bullwinkle protecting his little sister FiFi.

CHAPTER 9

NO ORDINARY DAY AT THE BEACH

It's 6:00 a.m. and there's a lot of activity at Monkey's House. Something exciting is about to happen. The pups can sense they are in for a special treat. Michele checks the weather, and for the middle of May, the weather is cooperating nicely for our trip. A beautiful day is predicted with a high around 70 degrees with a partly sunny sky. By all accounts, great spring weather for a day out with the entire crew.

As the aunts and uncles start to arrive, I'm making sure the accommodations within Waggin' One are ready for twenty-plus excited, howling dogs. Waggin' One was previously a senior citizen bus. Guess you can say it still is a senior bus, now just for dogs. One side of the bus has been equipped with shelves that were welded into place to ensure the dogs' utmost safety. This allows for three rows of crates—large on the bottom, medium in the middle, and small cross the top. I'm making sure each crate has a name tag for one of the dogs as well as a fresh, soft crate liner. On the other side of the bus are three bench seats that can accommodate six aunts or uncles. The bus came equipped with a wheelchair hydraulic lift; this comes in really handy for getting large dogs that can't walk into the bus. There's still room to fit a few strollers and a wagon in the back for those pups that need assistance on the beach.

All aboard Waggin' One for a fun excursion.

There's a fair amount of planning that goes into our larger field trips where all or most of the dogs are included. Weeks before the event, Michele will pick a couple of dates and get a consensus on the best one. Once the date is set and we know who is attending, the real planning begins. Michele is low-tech; she uses the old pencil-and-paper method to decide who will be transporting which pups and who is chauffeuring whom at the beach. When Michele asks who can drive, you might not want to raise your hand unless you don't mind being assigned as a stroller or wagon driver.

Since we've acquired Waggin' One, planning who is transporting the dogs has gotten much easier because most of them go in the bus. We may have one or two dogs travel in a car with their favorite aunt; their comfort is paramount to us. A large backseat might be just the thing, plus they avoid the singalongs that take place on the bus.

On this day, Joey, a large pit bull, will ride with Aunt Stacey. When Joey first came, we had him evaluated by a dog trainer to see how he interacted with other dogs. The evaluation showed he was not comfortable around a large number of dogs, so Aunt Stacey will handle him today. Aunt Stacey is well versed on dog obedience as she runs her own rescue, Happy Tails Rescue Retirement Home, and is a professional dog walker. Shadow, a black Lab, will travel with Aunt Kristen. Shadow loves all dogs and people; however, because of her very sore front legs, she will be more comfortable in a large backseat. It also helps that Aunt Kristen is one of her favorite aunts.

Planning who is walking which dog or dogs takes a little more thought than you might think. Michele's the guru on determining that, too. Like everything else that goes into supporting the Monkey's House dogs, there's a lot of common sense involved in making decisions, and the key is just really knowing the dogs. First, you determine who doesn't like who—dog, that is! Two dogs that don't care for one another can't be walked by the same person. Eve, aka Crazy Eve, is a good example as she hates Hooch. Obviously, they won't be walked together, and even on the walk, the aunts and uncles will need to keep that in mind and not walk them alongside one another. Then we think of speed; we pair up dogs with the same cadence whenever possible. If Oreo, a slow-walking poodle mix, is paired with Lucy, a fast-walking beagle, it just wouldn't be fair to Lucy. There's a lot of factors that go into pairing dogs, including what the aunt or uncle can handle, who can push a stroller in the sand, or who can keep up with a speedily walking dog such as Violet. All this planning takes place well before the big day, but we also have to be fluid to allow for last-minute changes the day of the trip.

With the dogs' early morning breakfast complete and all the aunts and uncles on the premises, it's time to load up the bus and cars. This moment reminds me of my elementary school field trips and all the excitement in the school parking lot as we entered the bus. The dogs are a lot like those third-graders. Pups are assigned to their person, and just as leashes are to be handed out, I jokingly shout out to the pups, "I need your signed permission slips to go on this trip!"

Today we're heading to the Jersey Shore, the dog beach in Brigantine to be more precise. It's just over an hour drive from our home and located right next to Atlantic City. Not five minutes out of our driveway the pups start singing. To me, it sounds a lot like a song we sang on our field trips but with a special twist. Apparently, they changed the lyrics of "The Wheels on the Bus Go Round-n-Round" to "The Dogs on the Bus Go Bow-Wow-Wow." I'll give them points for cleverness but not for harmony!

As we approach Atlantic City, we veer off to the left, driving right past a few of the major casinos. I get the feeling Eve, Hooch, and Maisey, the "wild bunch," would prefer to hit the casinos but not to-day; today is a beautiful day for the beach. We drive all the way to the northern tip of Brigantine and park in a large sand parking lot, which is perfect as I need a lot of room to maneuver Waggin' One. It's also a great staging area to get the strollers and wagon out and meet one of our forever fosters, Aunt Holly. Today, Aunt Holly brought the three Monkey's House pups that live with her, Bugsy, King, and Penelope (also known as El-O-Pee by her little boy Kaiden.)

Unloading the pups is a little tricky; the main thing is you don't want any getting loose. We actually leave the leashes on the cleverer ones when we travel just for this reason. The hydraulic lift comes in handy as we unload all the strollers and the wagon first. Hopefully, all the aunts and uncles remember their dog partners in crime they are assigned to. If not, Michele pulls out her handwritten notes, so we're cool!

Finally, it's off to the beach as we climb what seems like Mount Everest to the pups; up and over the sand dunes we go. I'm bringing up the rear making sure all's well in paradise, keeping an eye on those stroller drivers, Aunt Karen and Uncle Mike. The sand can get pretty deep and be hard to push a stroller through. That's called "sugar sand" in Southern Jersey. Looking ahead from the crest of the dune, I notice the one and only Melvin standing in his stroller like Leif Erikson, the Norse explorer from Iceland. However, unlike Erikson, who was the first-known European to have set foot on continental North America, Melvin thinks he's the first dog to set paws on Brigantine Beach. I didn't have the heart to tell him it's a "dog beach" and there's been thousands of dogs here over the years.

MELVIN AND "THE MELVIN SHOW"

Melvin had a roundabout way of getting to Monkey's House. Let's just say there were many hearts involved in his rescue and with his Aunt Rose bringing him here. She was about to adopt Melvin, but her veterinarian informed her of all his medical issues and recommended euthanasia instead. We're so thankful she reached out to us as the average person would find it hard to care for a dog with liver failure, a chronic cough, and serious heart issues complicated by very painful, infected teeth. He fit right in here; he discovered his final home. Melvin's story reminds me of one of my favorite songs I first heard a couple of years ago by the artist Sia, "Never Give Up." It basically says that you should never give up till you find your way home. Melvin may have been knocked to the ground, but he kept getting back up. If he was fighting to survive, we would never give up on him; we wouldn't let him down.

The first stop for Melvin when he arrived at Monkey's House was Dr. Morgan's office. From there, he had an ultrasound of his liver that showed a huge, angry liver but thankfully no signs of cancer. Next, he saw Dr. Michael Miller, our cardiologist. Medication was prescribed to slow down his racing heart, and other medications were prescribed to decrease the pressure in his lungs. Melvin's right-sided heart failure put tremendous strain on his liver. Dr. Miller felt Melvin would never be well enough for a dental procedure. Never say never to Michele! With food therapy, supportive herbs, and his heart meds, Melvin began to thrive. His liver enzymes returned to normal. He visited Dr. Miller a few months later and got the thumbs-up for a dental procedure. His mouth was a mess. Removing those infected teeth was a game changer for Melvin. He could finally eat without pain!

Dental disease is a terrible thing; it's the second-leading cause of pain in geriatric dogs, right behind arthritis.

Twice a day, we were privileged to witness the "Melvin Show." Every morning and evening, Melvin shared his opinions with us about his food, the bowl it was served in, the time, the taste—you name it, he had something to say about it. We quickly learned that in his opinion he was not a small dog. How dare we feed him in a small bowl! If LA and Sora, big dogs, were served with large bowls, then Melvin demanded a large bowl as well. You guessed it; his small amount of food was always served in our largest bowl.

Melvin may have looked like an ordinary Chihuahua, but once you got to know him, you quickly realized there was something quite extraordinary about this crusty, little old guy whose right eye was smaller than the left. He stole our hearts and was quite the ladies' man as he was generally seen with a "snuggle buddy" by his side. On this day at Brigantine Beach, Melvin was in his element. It was the "Melvin Show" on location, barking commands, leading the exploration.

As we stroll along the beach, the crew really spreads out. The fast-walkers are way up the beach. Aunt Karen is hanging near the water's edge not far from where we started pushing the "Dogger" stroller carrying Princess Granny and Cotton, with Maisey in tow.

Melvin was quite the ladies' man.

It's ironic that I'm walking the two cocker spaniels, Tequilla and Hooch, down the beach this beautiful day. Many times I've told Michele, no more cockers. All five that we've had at one point had or have a mind of their own. Michele calls it a "cockertude." I love these two guys, but they can be a handful at times. Luckily, today is not one of those days. They are both enjoying the water and all the smells along the beach. Tequilla is sniffing a large seaweed clump on the beach in wonder.

At one point, I was next to Michele who was walking Buck and Eve. On the beach, Eve was just plain Eve, no "Crazy" added to the front of her name today; she didn't go after Hooch once. Eve is blind, and I assume the ocean breeze and different smells threw off her senses that Hooch was nearby. As we both glanced over at Tequilla with the wind blowing through his hair, he was standing like a show dog ready to receive his ribbon. Michele softly said, "Look at Tequilla; there's a dog with no eyes enjoying a walk on the beach." As I turned toward Michele to add a verbal agreement, I saw she was becoming emotional. Realizing no words were needed, I lovingly squeezed her hand in acknowledgment.

TEQUILLA—BLIND AND FRIENDLY

Tequilla made his way to Monkey's House because his owners were moving and didn't want to take him to their new home, so they took him to a local kill shelter. We couldn't imagine the fear he must have been subjected to. Besides the severe pain from the horrific mats of hair over his body, including his long, hairy cocker ears, he had a severe heart murmur. For the most part, he was blind as well. The shelter had him slated to be destroyed. I'm sure it's hard for you to even imagine that being old, neglected, and slightly imperfect carries a death sentence! Our good friends from Tiny Paws Rescue were at the shelter that day and noticed the horrible shape Tequilla was in. Even though he was to be euthanized that evening, they felt it important to clean him up and remove all the hurtful mats. He deserved to feel good

Tequilla enjoying a walk on the beach.

one last time, to have some of his dignity back. In the process, they realized what a wonderful dog he was, and although Tiny Paws Rescue couldn't take him, they thought he was a good candidate for Monkey's House and called Michele.

Boy, were our friends right. Tequilla is one of the friendliest dogs we've ever had. He loves everybody, even people he meets for the first time. One of his favorite pastimes is to sit on a lap and give out kisses all day and night. For an older dog, he also has a good amount of energy. He's one of my favorite dogs to take on long walks. You might wonder how he could be a good walker if he's blind. It all comes down to trust. If the dog trusts you and you start taking walks, you can guide the dog with the leash. Over time, that trust will build like it did for Tequilla with me. You have to remember to pay attention; don't accidently walk a blind dog into a pole, a tree, or off a curb!

Shortly after arriving here, Tequilla had to have his left eye removed because of painful glaucoma; then six months later, the other eye had the same fate. Michele took him to see a specialist to see if the eye could be saved and whether he had any vision, but as she assumed his vision couldn't be restored. Since the eye was causing him immense pain, we made the decision to have it removed.

With a healthy diet and the proper medication, his heart murmur did not get any worse. He has no exercise restrictions.

As Tequilla walks on the beach, we are reminded that having a disability doesn't mean inability. He has the ability to enjoy a walk on the beach. Many of us have disabilities. Don't let it stop you from taking your "walk on the beach."

As the lead walker turns and heads back to meet up with the tail end of the group, the others are picked up along the way and eventually we all congregate. The pups are tired out; well most, anyway. I do think Violet can go another few miles if we'd let her (more on Violet in chapter 14, "The Journey Forward"). I grab a young man nearby and ask him to snap some pictures for us. After I explain to him the mission of Monkey's House, he's more than willing to take group shots with my phone.

No ordinary day at the beach, Brigantine, NJ, 2019.

We had a nice time on the beach; everyone seemed to enjoy themselves. Time to load everybody back up to go home. It's a little easier loading the dogs up to go home as there's not as much energy left in them because they're all tuckered out. I think the aunts and uncles are worn out as well. There will probably be no singing on the way home; what a shame! Our estimated arrive time at home is a little before 11:30 a.m. Our trips are not long; we want to give the dogs a good outing without stressing their already weakened bodies.

After arriving home, the pups seem to have a Zen aura about them. We can tell they enjoyed the outing as did all the aunts and uncles. As the last aunt pulls out of the driveway, Michele and I get a chance to plop down in the family room for a short break. Michele is on the sofa with five pups nestled around her, and I'm sitting in a lounge chair with a couple on my lap. The other pups have all claimed their spots in comfy beds throughout the room. Hooch catches my attention; he appears to be dreaming, no doubt of catching some waves on his banana surfboard.

All is well in the Monkey House universe at this moment.

CHAPTER 10

SOFA MEDICINE:
"KEEPING IT NORMAL"

> *In an ideal world, there would be no need for a Monkey's House.*
> *All dogs would live out their lives with their pet parents. Sadly,*
> *we know our society in its entirety has not gotten to this point.*
> *Our dream is just that—a hopeful dream that will someday*
> *come to fruition.*

A critical component of our mission is to not only rescue homeless hospice dogs but also teach pet parents that they can manage end-of-life care for their beloved pets at home. I don't think anybody expects it to be easy. I believe most people lack the confidence and are fearful of what lies ahead. Michele's personal mission is to guide those with doubts, provide them with knowledge, and give them the tools they need so their desire to make their pups a priority becomes a reality. You do not need a medical background to develop basic skills that will enable you to care for your ailing dog. These skills, along with a good relationship with your veterinarian, will go a long way in making the care more manageable and less stressful, allowing you (and your pet) to actually enjoy the twilight of its life.

Once your pet gets into its golden years and starts to need more medical attention, many pet parents may begin to think, "Oh, no; not another trip to the vet; he'll get stressed out," or you might become beset by a slew of questions such as: "How do I fit this into my busy schedule?" "Where do I find the money?" "Am I really capable of doing this?"

First and foremost, educate yourself about your dog's condition to facilitate more productive conversations with your veterinarian. Is your veterinarian comfortable in guiding you through procedures to care for your pet? Can he or she refer you to other resources in your area? With the proper knowledge, there are many actions you can take within the confines of your own home. Knowledge is the great equalizer; it will help alleviate your concerns over your pet's stress, time constraints, and expense worries. At this stage, wouldn't you rather be focused on your dog, not "distractions" that will likely impact your pet's health as well as yours? In chapter 3, I talked about the power of positive thinking, the energy it creates. Your goal should be to keep a positive attitude; your dog will sense your energy. Most important, provide unconditional love, like the love they've given *you* their entire lives.

"Sofa Medicine" is what you need. Michele coined this term; it refers to different treatments you can do at home, in many cases while sitting right on your sofa with your pup. Michele stresses that the first and one of the most important things you need is a good relationship with your veterinarian; if you don't have this, it's time to find a new veterinarian. Your veterinarian needs to be in sync with you on your pet's health and well-being. You need to have confidence in not only his or her abilities but also that your wishes are understood. Because Monkey's House is unique, we use a variety of veterinarians and specialists. Michele has gone through a few so-called specialists she wouldn't even recommend to a cat parent! (Sorry, Grandpa, only kidding on the cat reference.) Seriously, you wouldn't settle for a doctor for your own health, don't settle for on a veterinarian for your pets. At Monkey's House, we take a comprehensive approach to medicine and thus want our professionals to see the advantages of both traditional and nontraditional veterinary medicine. If you feel the same way and have a traditional veterinarian, be sure he or she is open to nontraditional alternatives.

From your sofa, you can administer an array of treatments depending on your dog's medical conditions. In celebrating Parker's, Pumpkin's, FiFi's, and Murphy's lives, a few of the procedures we used and continue to use at home include the following

+ B12 Shots: used to help reverse anemia in dogs with chronic conditions or bleeding disorders.
+ Chinese Herbal Supplement (Yunnan Baiyao): used with bleeding cancers such as hemangiosarcoma in promoting blood clotting during bleeds. Also used during any kind of bleeding emergency and before surgeries.
+ Insulin: regulates blood sugar levels in diabetic dogs.
+ Nausea Medication (Cerenia): medication given to dogs to help treat and prevent vomiting.
+ Nebulizer Treatments: helps open the airways of a dog with pneumonia or kennel cough.
+ Oxygen Therapy: supplementing oxygen intake with dogs having breathing difficulties.
+ Seizure Medication (Valium Suppositories, Midazolam): these drugs help in sedating or slowing brain activity in dogs that are seizing. This slowing of the brain activity is helpful since the brain is overactive when a dog is having a seizure.
+ Subcutaneous Fluids (Sub Q Fluids): supplemental fluids for dogs with kidney disease or dehydration.

PARKER, THE "MAYOR OF MONKEY'S HOUSE"

One night, as I pulled the car up to the house, I noticed a lot of activity in the Cottage. Peering through the window, I could see Michele working with a dog. I was not sure which dog it was because it was out of my line of sight. As I strolled into the Healing Room to say hello to Michele, I saw her giving fluids to a new resident, a pit bull. The first words out of my mouth, half-jokingly, were, "What, a pit bull?!"

Michele quickly snapped back, "Get over it."

Truthfully, I had never interacted with a pit bull, and with the bad publicity they get, I was a little insecure. Michele introduced me to Parker, and from that moment on I've come to realize that "pitties," an endearing term for pit bulls, are just like any other dog— four legs of love!

South Jersey Regional Animal Shelter picked Parker up from the side of the road and took him to Voorhees Animal Orphanage. Emaciated and shivering, the staff got him to their veterinarian right away. Twenty-four hours later, they were given crushing news: Parker was in total renal failure. All the veterinarian could recommend was humane euthanasia. That was a heavy blow for their staff and volunteers; in less than twenty-four hours, they had their hearts stolen by this adorable guy. The kennel manager, Laurie Ballard, contacted Michele to see if we could offer any hope. We took Parker in and promised we would try our best.

Parker's body was fading fast; he was anemic and his blood work was in dire condition. We could tell he wanted to stay alive, so we did all we could to help him. While he was busy giving kisses and wagging his tail, we were busy giving him small frequent meals that would support his weakened kidneys and help build his strength to improve his mobility. Hydration was key as was keeping him warm so his body temperature wouldn't drop. Finally, and most important, we assured Parker he was loved. We never know how a dog's story will end or how long they have. What we do know is they are deeply loved while they are here at Monkey's House.

We put Parker on a home-cooked diet for his renal failure that avoided foods with ingredients that were hard for his kidneys to eliminate. He also got sub Q fluids twice a day, morning and night. Parker improved beyond our wildest dreams in just a few weeks. At that point he wasn't out of the woods yet, but we could see the light shining brightly through the trees at the end of the forest. We were thrilled that Parker was blessed with more time.

All we hope for these hospice dogs is time to show them love, to let them know they matter. No dog should face their dying days homeless. We work at warp speed to make what little time they have with us incredible.

Administering supplemental fluids can benefit dogs with a variety of medical conditions. The most common use of fluid therapy, *sub Q fluids*, is for dogs with kidney disease or *chronic renal failure (CRF)* like Parker. Michele has also administered fluids on dogs with other medical conditions as needed. If your dog is diagnosed with a condition that could benefit from fluid therapy, ask your veterinarian to teach you how to perform this simple procedure. Don't be afraid; I learned to administer fluids and I don't have a medical background. At first, I felt apprehensive about the process. I believe most laymen probably feel that way. Giving injections was outside of my comfort zone, but once I was properly taught how to do it, it really wasn't that difficult. Things I've thought I could never do have become commonplace, especially when it's saving one of my dogs' lives and keeping them home and comfortable. The benefits to your dog make it well worth the effort to learn this simple technique.

Parker was truly the first "rock star" of Monkey's House. All the dogs that make their way here are special, but every once in a while, we get one that really tugs on the Monkey's House family's hearts. Parker was that special guy. He blossomed here, and although his mobility was very limited, he would quickly go up to visitors offering them his toys. Parker was very expressive and he just loved people! He hated getting his sub Q fluids but cooperated for our sake. He loved rubs of all kinds—belly, neck, whatever. But one of his favorite activities was napping in the sun. On the days when he didn't feel like eating, he would take a few bites when we hand-fed him just to please us.

"The Mayor of Monkey's House," that was the nickname I gave Parker. Besides loving people, he got along great with all the other

Parker, our loving and lovable "pittie."

dogs. He would travel back and forth between the Cottage and main house on a daily basis so he got to visit with all the other dogs. Parker had a standing appointment at 2 p.m. in the main house to watch *Little House on the Prairie*. He was fascinated with that TV show and demanded that everybody be quiet when it was on. Lil, a little four-pound Chihuahua, would always lay next to him. I think she was Parker's personal protection dog. He always felt safe when his friend Lil was on duty; she had his back.

Parker was opinionated, so much so the "Mayor" decided to run for president in 2016. He was garnering a lot of support across the country. The political establishment took notice and before we knew it, stories were circulating about Parker's excessive liquor addiction. The press labeled it "Liquor-Gate." After a thorough investigation, it turned out they misrepresented the facts. Parker did have a serious problem; he freely admitted he couldn't hold his "LICKER"! He never missed the opportunity to plant a big, long kiss on anyone who was in range. Parker decided to take a break from politics to enjoy bully sticks while basking in the sun.

For nine months, Parker stole our hearts at Monkey's House; his joy and zest for life was awesome and inspiring. He enjoyed bully sticks, marrow bones, laying on the furniture, sleeping in the sunshine, belly rubs...lots and lots of belly rubs. When it was Parker's time to make his way to the Rainbow Bridge, we made sure it was in one of his favorite locations, a beautiful spot in our front yard where he had enjoyed many a belly rub. We put down a soft comfy bed, had heating pads and a blanket to keep him warm on that cold December day. We were grateful for the bright sunshine on his face; he was surrounded by love. Knowing and loving Parker was a true honor and privilege for us.

OUR ADORABLE PUMPKIN—A REAL STUFFED ANIMAL

Before Pumpkin came to Monkey's House, I would occasionally see a picture of an adorable Pomeranian on social media. I swore they weren't real. They were just too cute; they looked like stuffed animals. Now I can tell you they are real; Pumpkin was living proof. He was the cutest little Pomeranian and lived up to his name with a coat that matched the color of a pumpkin.

To go along with a laundry list of medical issues, his gravest was a cancerous mass on the top of the right side of his heart, called *hemangiosarcoma*. It would spontaneously bleed from time to time. Pumpkin would be fine and then suddenly he would collapse and then be somewhat unresponsive for six to twelve hours. During that time, we would administer *Yunnan Baiyao* (a Chinese herb to stop the bleeding). We would hold him until he started to be himself again. This happened quite a few times during his nine months with us. A dog's life expectancy with hemangiosarcoma is cut extremely short, generally less than three months. We believe this Chinese supplement stopped many of his bleeds and gave him a good three seasons with us at Monkey's House, fall, winter, and spring. In that short amount of time with us, he had more lives than a cat.

A little dog that was abandoned outside of a kill shelter, laying in his bed next to a busy highway, Pumpkin was spotted by a guardian angel who scooped him up, and he eventually made his way to us via our great partner, Tiny Paws Rescue. Their veterinarian determined that Pumpkin had multiple medical issues, was not adoptable, and recommended euthanasia.

Nine months was more than enough time for Pumpkin to make a great impression on not only the Monkey's House family but also

Pumpkin was much more demanding but much
more adorable than a cute stuffed animal!

all who met him or read of his antics. When Michele had veterinary
appointments, Pumpkin would often go along for the ride. She said it
was to keep the other dogs company, but I think Michele knew how
much Pumpkin loved people and enjoyed seeing the veterinary staff,
his extended family. He adored all of the love and attention. You could
see the look on his face like, "Yeah, the chicks dig me, I'm adorable,
yada, yada, yada."

My one special memory of Pumpkin was his zest for dinner. Preparing meals at our house is not a quick endeavor; it can take upward
of an hour and a half as each dog gets a tailored meal for its optimal
health. Pumpkin would wait as long as he could, but the excitement
would overtake him to the point where he would firmly tell us it was
taking too long. The energy would build within him, and he just
had to complain with a bark. No just an ordinary bark, but one that
would levitate his entire body off the ground. After a twenty-second
recharge, he would let us have it again! This tiny guy would crack me
up. I remember promising him I would let the whole world know of
his bad manners. Pumpkin, I guess I just did. Love you, little guy.

FIFI—A MIRACLE DOG

FiFi is another dog that has convinced me that miracles do happen. Michele really isn't just some "crazy dog lady." She's the magic behind many of the miracles we've witnessed, of course, along with the help from our wonderful team of veterinarians and specialists. This little sixteen-year-old poodle was surrendered to Philly ACCT after her pet parent had died. We received a call from the shelter urgently asking us to take her right away; she was on the brink of dying. Transport brought her to Monkey's House lethargic, covered in blood and urine. After assessing FiFi, Michele rushed her to Dr. Morgan's office. It was determined she was diabetic and was in *diabetic ketosis-acidosis* (DKA). She also had a blood infection from badly infected teeth and was extremely dehydrated. Although things were dire for FiFi, she didn't outwardly seem to be suffering. We were sure FiFi was missing her mom; her head was drooped in sorrow; she wouldn't even look up. Michele said, "Something inside me just felt like she wanted to live, and we were determined to help her as long as she was up to fighting."

That evening, our downstairs bathroom was transformed into a mini-ICU complete with equipment we had either acquired or borrowed from Dr. Morgan's office. FiFi received IV fluids and IV antibiotics while being held by Michele day and night. Her blood sugar levels were monitored and the insulin regulated accordingly. It was very touch and go for a few days. I wasn't sure Michele was going to be able to save her; the odds were not in FiFi's favor. Several times her blood sugar spiked to 750; the normal range is between 80 and 100. On the fourth day after FiFi joined us, I came home from work and saw a little poodle trotting around the kitchen island. I was shocked when I realized it was FiFi. Besides the medical care we administered, we truly believe being held and loved those crucial days helped FiFi get through this terrible time in her life.

Clearly, she was doing much better, yet she wasn't out of the woods. Managing her blood sugar levels was quite challenging as it is with any diabetic, especially in the early stages when you are trying to figure out the proper insulin dose. We had to learn how her body responded to the insulin, so we kept a very close eye on her. We were well prepared with both insulin and maple syrup in the refrigerator door to counteract both high- and low-blood sugar levels.

The other pups would even lend a hand at keeping an eye on FiFi. One night, Bea started barking and screaming. Michele ran downstairs to find FiFi standing on top of Bea, acting confused. Michele checked FiFi's blood sugar, and it had dropped to 22. It was an easy fix with syrup and a little food. This happened to her from time to time but on this night, it was a really close call. Thank God she found a way to ask for help. Bea was the hero that night and was awarded the official role of "screaming loudly to get Mom up in the middle of the night."

FiFi lived life to the fullest. It's like when you go through an extremely rough path and are able to come out stronger and more determined to enjoy every day. Early on, we learned that FiFi loved hugs. I mean she really would give you a hug that you would get from a true love. She would wrap her front legs around your neck and pull herself in close. They say you should get plenty of hugs in a day to live a fulfilled life. FiFi helped us achieve that for sure.

Please include plans for your pets in your will. Give your executor the name of your dog walker/sitter, family and friends who would be willing to help. FiFi lost her person, was frightened, sick, and then nearly lost her life,

FiFi, our miracle pup, soft as a baby lamb.

and not in a "they were meant to be together" kind of way, but from neglect and lack of the proper veterinary care. We were so glad to have FiFi as part of our family for well over two years and be able to rewrite the final chapter of her life's story. Please don't risk the unthinkable happening to your pets.

"MAD DOG" MURPHY

Murphy, aka "Mad Dog" Murphy, had his own law. It wasn't the old adage, "Anything that can go wrong, will go wrong." it was more like, "Any trouble he could get into, he would get into." This mischievous Pomeranian mix acted more like a puppy than the senior dog that came to us in congestive heart failure (CHF) and a mouth full of broken, rotten teeth. With medication his heart condition stabilized. The next stop was on to Dr. Morgan's office for his neuter and dental procedure, also known as the Tuesday special—"Testicles and Teeth." He had twenty-five teeth removed, a record for Monkey's House that still stands today. Murphy also had some wild hair. As soon as he was on the mend, we had to do something with that '80s hair. We took him to see his Aunt Floss of Floss's Grooming. Who knew he was so dapper under all that hair?

Within a few months, we noticed something was a little off with Murphy. He was diagnosed with *pulmonary hypertension*, but some adjustments with his medications had him back to his troublemaking self in no time. Murphy loved playing with the other dogs. He would even try to engage those dogs that opted not to play in a little horseplay. He was living larger than life. Sadly, however, his CHF returned with a vengeance. We knew all too well about CHF as it had taken many dogs from us, including our precious Monkey.

One day, Aunt Sandi heard Murphy coughing. He did that quite often as his enlarged heart would irritate his windpipe. She went to check on him and found him having a full grand mal seizure (a *grand mal seizure* is a whole body seizure that causes your dog's entire body to convulse). She held him lovingly through the seizure, but then he went limp and was having trouble breathing. Michele listened to his heart and lungs and gave him emergency diuretics. Aunt Sandi grabbed Mary Poppins as Michele sent an urgent text to Dr. Morgan. Within ten minutes, Michele, with Dr. Morgan's guidance, devised a homemade oxygen tent out of a crate and Saran Wrap. Oxygen was pumping in from the oxygen concentrator that was in Mary Poppins's magical bag. Shortly after being put in the tent, the medications started to take effect, and Murphy went from limp and gasping for air to bright-eyed and eating a fish stick. We left the oxygen tent set up and used it for him on several more occasions. We were surprised at Murphy's willingness to go into the handmade oxygen tent.

Murphy's days were filled with adventure, a bit of trouble, and lots of love. We enjoyed his company for ten months; we were hoping for

Murphy ready to get into some mischief.

more. But thankfully, we had more than enough time to show him the kinder side of humanity. In his last days, it was getting harder for Murphy to breathe, and his little stays in the oxygen tent were no longer making a difference. The mobile veterinary service, HousePaws, came to Monkey's House. In my arms with Michele next to him giving him a lot of love and kisses, he made his way to the Rainbow Bridge.

While Michele's nursing background makes caring for a hospice dog much easier than for someone who does not have a medical background, let me reiterate that you don't need to be a nurse or have medical experience to provide some level of care at home. However, as I've also said before, I do stress you need to work closely with your veterinarian. And just to remind you, I don't have a medical background, and I've learned to give insulin shots, sub Q fluids, provide oxygen, and aid a dog during and after a seizure. I can pretty much handle most issues. When I hit a wall, I reach out to the experts, first asking Michele for guidance or our veterinarian when needed. Hospice care can be a beautiful gift for those dogs with end-stage diseases. So much can be done on your sofa in a surrounding familiar to the pup, putting both you and your dog at ease in a loving setting, what we like to call, "keeping it normal."

CHAPTER 11

CELEBRATION OF LIFE

When MLBob passed, our global family was devastated with his loss. We received many heartfelt comments on social media from our Monkey's House family in celebration of this little beagle's life that was loved by so many. Michele reminded everyone that there were a lot more dogs that needed their love. She said, "Pass the 'red balloon,' pass the love of MLBob to another pup." We started to see the red balloon icon everywhere. Folks acknowledged that they were passing their love on to the other Monkey's House dogs. It was wonderful to see. In that vein, I wanted to share a little poem I wrote, "The Red Balloon."

"THE RED BALLOON"

A red balloon signifies hope,
Hope to be cherished and loved.
Our dogs once gazed through steel bars
Void of love, they were tossed.
By some miracle, they find their way home,
A home inspired by a little dog named Monkey.
Given love and dignity they shine,
Making every moment count,
Even at their final breath.
Thankful for the love they received,
The love of Monkey's House grows.

It's time to pass the red balloon,
To another pup in need.
Passing the love that never fades,
The love that only grows,
Pass the red balloon.

EASYGOING LA

Every dog that comes to Monkey's House goes through a period of adjustment. That was no exception for LA, a large yellow Lab-pit bull mix. No matter how good the food is, how kind we are, how soft the beds, any change for a dog is stressful. Sometimes, it takes weeks before dogs have free run of the house. LA was the creakiest and bumpiest old dog we've ever seen. She was incredibly sweet and willing to trust, although her body tells us she had plenty of reasons to be neither. Early on, she spent the bulk of her time out in the Cottage with Shadow. It was her safe place in a new environment. The Cottage is quiet, warm, and peaceful, and Shadow was good company with her gentle, calm demeanor. The radio plays, the beds are super-comfy, and the sunlight coming through the windows is very healing.

After a couple of weeks, LA started to venture into the main house for brief supervised visits. While she loved her visits, she did start panting after spending just a tiny amount of time there, so we were easing her into her visits with short stays. After a week of her spending time with the entire crew, one day she just laid down on the floor of the main house. For a new dog who is feeling a bit stressed, this is a big deal. Within minutes, Leo, another dog that was terrified when he first came here, was at her side gently licking her face. It was an honor to witness such a tender, loving moment.

Within the first two weeks, Michele took LA to see Dr. Morgan for a thorough exam. The results showed that her spleen was gigantic; she had *hemangiosarcoma*, a form of cancer of the blood vessels. Her spleen was at risk of rupturing, a life-threatening situation. She was also severely arthritic, had an array of lumps and bumps that looked menacing, dental issues, and had never been spayed. We put LA on some additional supplements, continued her healthy fresh diet, and quickly scheduled a follow-up appointment for surgery to remove her spleen and to be spayed. The surgery was successful. While under anesthesia, they also performed a dental procedure to remove her many rotten and broken teeth. Besides being painful, rotten, infected teeth seem to escalate all chronic health issues, especially heart problems. LA came away with a beautiful set of choppers. Dr. Morgan is quick and meticulous with her surgeries; still, we decided to leave her lumps and bumps alone at that time. Her spleen was our main focus. As for the hemangiosarcoma, we eventually found out that it had spread. She would have an occasional bleed, and like Pumpkin, she was given the *Yunnan Baiyao* to stop the bleeding.

LA was very easygoing and made friends with all the other pups. She had her own very large bed and was more than willing to share it with a pup, or two, or three. There wasn't a mean bone in this girl's body. LA asked almost nothing of us, except when we were making dinner, then manners and decorum flew out the window. LA moved to the front of the line—it was every pup for herself!

Most of us have a favorite place in our homes. Maybe it's a particular room or a special chair. LA's favorite place was the front porch. She absolutely loved the fresh air and sun on her face. Generally, if it weren't a rainy day, LA was on the porch; she would settle for the back deck in a pinch, but the front was her preference. The front of the house faces directly south, and the rays of the sun are the strongest there. They shone on her beautiful face. In the winter, she refused to listen to us telling her it was too cold to be outside. Next thing you know, I'm putting down extra bedding, sticking the portable heat packs in the microwave. As we helped her snuggle under the covers with heat packs all around, you could see the contentment on her beautiful face highlighted by the sun. One of our global family members, Aunt Patricia, sent an outdoor heated fleece blanket that LA loved. On many a day, you would see the hens visiting LA or catch Grandpa laying with her.

Like a couple of kindred souls, they were just rockin' it out on the front porch, sharing a giant marrow bone or a bowl of warm bone broth.

We took LA to PetPt to see if we could improve her mobility and to make sure we were doing our best for her. Her body was a mess; we knew that already, and time was not on her side; it never had been. However, the love, energy, and magic that is Monkey House was behind her 100 percent. She was examined by Dr. Russell Howe-Smith, a rehabilitation and pain management specialist at PetPT. He explained what was going on with her knees, hips, and muscle loss...and at some point, without moving a muscle, she stole his heart as well.

He felt she would benefit from the treadmill but wasn't sure she was really up to it. Nothing about her was typical or predictable. We gave it a try. Well, LA lit up, energized by the love surrounding her, and she gave it her all and did extremely well. The water in the treadmill lifted the weight off her old, arthritic joints, and the slow but steady underwater moving belt helped her walk with a steady gait. In this case, one of the awesome technicians, Cody, actually sat in the water with her, moving her hind legs in the correct, rhythmical motion. She loved it.

Next was the cold laser; she loved that as well. She came home all tuckered out. Anyone who has ever been laid up for any length of time knows that joyous feeling when you are tired from doing something, anything, that resembles your old, independent self. As I've said, we did all we could for her. We didn't think there was anything about her body we could truly fix, but we were confident we had healed her soul. We made every day she had with us the best it could be. We all doted on her, kept her warm, clean, and comfortable and made sure she knew how important she was, how beautiful she was, and how deeply she was loved. Her life was important.

If you recall the sitcom *Cheers*, every time one of the characters, Norm, walked into the bar, everybody would shout his name, "Norm," as a form of hello. At Monkey's House, when an aunt or uncle arrives, we break into song (let me clarify, the dogs break into song, not Michele or me). Aunt Claire is a morning person and comes to help out with the dogs a few mornings a week. When she comes in, she heads right into the family room and takes a seat. This helps the dogs stay calm and gives her time to say good morning to them all. Mind you, this is done with a deafening "singing" that's taking place. LA, who almost never gets up for anybody, always made her way to say good morning to one of her favorite aunts.

LA prepared for a nice sunny day.

Aunt Claire is also one of our cooks. You can catch her on many days with twenty-five pounds of turkey or beef being gently cooked for the next few days' feedings. When Aunt Claire was in the kitchen, a special blanket would be put down on the floor at her feet so that LA could be close to her. I'm not sure if LA was hoping the cook was sloppy with some food droppings coming her way, or if she was making sure the food was cooked to her liking. We know she loved Aunt Claire, but I wouldn't have put it past LA to have those other things on her mind, too.

Those lumps and bumps we mentioned earlier, one suddenly grew in size and would spontaneously bleed. It needed to be removed. Sadly, the pathology report disclosed an aggressive form of cancer, a *mast cell tumor*. There is nothing positive I can say about this type of cancer. What I will say is that we loved LA and were deeply vested in her comfort and happiness. How many of us have someone consciously making plans to make sure we are happy, comfortable, and feeling loved every day? This is hospice life—living, loving, and being in the moment. Tomorrow isn't promised to any of us. For little over a year, LA had LIVED her final chapter with us. She passed away quietly and gently in the early hours of the morning. She loved so deeply; we feel this is the way she wanted it, not having to look into our eyes and say good-bye; she loved us too much. See you on the other side, LA. I can only imagine how fast you'll run up to greet us all.

If you're a pet parent, sooner or later the day will come when you have to say good-bye to your best friend until that time you meet again. None of us want to think of that day, but if you have a senior dog, it's best to have a conversation with your veterinarian. He or she can provide you with an array of possibilities and reference material. If you're not a planner, this is the one time you want to be one. It will allow you and your dog to enjoy the remaining time together and not worry about the process.

Michele has had many of our Monkey's House family reach out to her, some looking for advice on their dog's end-of-life care while others are looking for comfort and solidarity. Sadly, there were a few who fell into another category altogether. They experienced great sorrow for the loss of their dogs and were viewing that final day with deep heartache and anguish.

One such person was a new pet parent. She so loved having her first dog and they had a good life together. When that dreaded day came, she took Clover to the vet's office, talked to the receptionist, and left when Clover went back to get assisted to the Rainbow Bridge. She didn't know she could have been with Clover during the procedure, providing him comfort to his final journey. She was devastated, not once but twice. Losing her best friend was bad enough, but not being there for him in his time of need was horrible, an experience she regrets to this day.

Another person had dogs her entire life, and when it was Missy's time, she did everything she thought was right. She was there holding Missy as she was assisted to the Rainbow Bridge. When asked if she wanted to take Missy home to bury her or have her cremated, she said the town didn't allow burials so she told them to cremate her. In her time of sorrow, she didn't realize there's two types of cremations, group and individual. Missy was cremated with other animals and she never received Missy's ashes. Another mom who regretted that day for more reasons than one.

Michele calls the day your best friend makes its way to the Rainbow Bridge "the day nobody wants to talk about." Truthfully, she'll tell you it's not just that day but the days, weeks, and months leading up to it that are difficult. We have to rely on our veterinarians' advice, but it's important to remember that they only see our pets for very short periods of time. Their advice will be based on general veterinary principles. As pet parents, we know our dogs better than anyone else in the world; we're with them day in and day out.

Educate yourself on the process, find out what that final day will entail, and what all the options are. Do you want your pet's final goodbye to be in the veterinary office, or do you want a home euthanasia? We have a veterinarian come to Monkey's House. We believe that's where our dogs are most comfortable, surrounded by familiarity and the ones they love, even other pets. We let the other dogs see the process and get to say their good-byes. This is a very personal decision that we'll all need to make. Just be well-informed of the possibilities.

A FINAL WORD ABOUT DAISY MAE

Although I've already told Daisy Mae's story in chapter 4, "Whatever It Takes," I felt Michele's quote about her final day belonged here:

> *"When Daisy's time came, we knew everything went as it should and that her final gift to us, a smile after struggling to breathe all day, was a beautiful miracle in and of itself. Just as we strive to show how exceptionally wonderful life can be with dogs as their time gets small, we would like to show that their loss is something we can bear. Like most pet parents, you may have a headache or fogginess for days, eyes burning (from all the tears you shed), not believing they are gone. Even in multiple-dog families you'll miss their presence. We feel the loss for a long time; the house feels empty and we generally have twenty-five dogs. You'll cry and relive their final day and question your every decision even though you're okay with your choice. It's all a normal part of grieving. Losing Daisy Mae, like (losing) any of our dogs, was tough. If you have never lost a dog, it is as bad as everyone says, but it's survivable. Reach out if you need to, the days do get better. They are always worth the pain and heartache; love is all-powerfully healing."*

All of our dogs are buried on the farm. I have a very special spot overlooking the pond and our house. It's just off the final turn home from our pack walks in our back field. Many times, aunts are here with us to see off their beloved friends and ask if I want help. I always reply, "No thanks, I'll be fine." I've never really told them this is my time, my final farewell. I find myself saying a little prayer as they are wrapped in a prayer blanket in their final resting place. I can't really put my finger on it; it's such a peaceful time for me. Could it be because I know we did the right thing, giving this dog a good final chapter? My senses are keen at this moment. A couple of folks commented that Bea was their little flower. When I laid her to rest and turned to go home, I noticed one little flower, out of hundreds of daylilies that line our pond, had bloomed early. Or I'll notice a bluebird landing on the fence or a beautiful sunset.

I would like to think our beloved pups are saying, "Thank you for loving and caring for us," as they make their way to heaven.

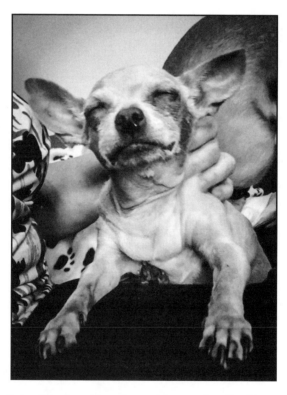

Daisy Mae loved her time with us to her final hour.

CHAPTER 12

IS SANTA REAL?

Michele and I have had a lot of children, not your "normal" children, but the ones with fur, hair, or feathers. Like a typical family, we like to have a family portrait taken around Christmas with Santa. The first year we had Monkey—this was pre-Monkey's House—our wacky but heartfelt tradition started. A local shelter called the Voorhees Animal Orphanage puts on an annual fund-raiser where you can get a photo taken with Santa—dogs are not optional, people are. This photo-op takes place at a high-end strip mall called the Promenade located in Voorhees, New Jersey.

Michele is friends with many of the shelter's staff members and volunteers. We've rescued and fostered many dogs from the Voorhees Animal Orphanage, including Monkey. Michele gave them advance notice that the entire Allen family was attending, all eight of us. If you do the math, that makes six dogs inside an Orvis store. At the time, that was a lot of dogs to control in an unfamiliar setting. (Today, we would be like, "only six?")

We had a game plan, or maybe I should say I had a plan. As we drove into the mall parking lot, I remember stressing that we had to keep to the plan. Michele acknowledged me, but I also believe I noticed some eye rolling, and it wasn't from the dogs! This plan entailed a mathematical equation that determined that two of the smallest dogs would go on Santa's lap; he wouldn't mind; all Santas love dogs, right? Michele would have the larger dogs on the floor in front of her, and I would hold Monkey and have another on the floor. My *A* personality was shining through on this day as I thought, piece of cake.

Just like everybody else, we had to wait in line with pups in tow. I was so worried our pups would make a scene, maybe pee on a clothing rack or start "ruff"-housing." But they were all very well-behaved (luckily, we didn't have Mr. Peebody yet).

As we got closer to Santa, we were getting ready to jump into action. It felt like the *Seinfeld* episode where they were getting ready to order soup from the Soup Nazi. Next thing you know, it's our turn. Go, go, go! As we charged Santa, to his surprise, Michele tossed the first pup onto his lap. (I guess in retrospect we should have included Santa in on our game plan.) But Santa *was* a jolly old sport and adjusted the pup on his lap. Michele didn't have the nerve to give him another one, so our plans changed a little as we took our positions next to Santa, smiled and said cheese, and voila, we had our first family portrait with Santa. This was a great adventure and experience that we will treasure forever. The pups had a blast, and we had just started a new annual tradition.

Annual events can be a lot of fun, but you always look for ways to outdo the previous year, and our pictures with Santa were no exception. Our second year, we added three more dogs for a total of nine. Let me explain: We didn't just find an additional three dogs for the photo, but over the year we ended up with a few more fosters. But more dogs are just that, more dogs, so what? Well, that wasn't good enough; I thought, let's dress them all in holiday attire, too.

Michele started to add her two cents to the game plan. With her input, I was back to designing the plan: Santa holds two dogs; Michele holds two dogs with two dogs on the floor; and I'll hold Monkey with two dogs on the floor. This time Santa saw us coming, he recognized Michele, and was ready for the tossed-up dogs. All we needed was a little staging help from our friends from the shelter, and we'd be golden. The dogs were angels as they quickly got into position and smiled for the camera as we heard, "Say cheese." We couldn't believe how good the picture came out. What a great holiday photo!

The second year we took our holiday photo with Santa. Monkey is on my lap.
Photo courtesy of James Balga

The third year we took our holiday photo with Santa, we were officially Monkey's House. We were at fifteen dogs. Frankly, I didn't think Santa could catch and hold five dogs. So, we enlisted a few aunts and uncles to be in the photo holding dogs. This shoot was difficult, but not because of the pups; they were well-behaved. The room was a little too small for us, and as we waited for the signal to smile, there was an issue with the camera. Just imagine trying to keep fifteen dogs staged for what seemed like ten minutes. In the end, we had another nice picture and great memories.

By the fourth year it was like clockwork. I hate to say it, but Michele benched me and took over the role of master planner. Since we now had twenty-six dogs, planning started weeks before. Michele had to think about transport vehicles, which aunts and uncles would attend, Christmas outfits, wagons for those that needed a ride from the car to the store, and medical supplies in case of emergency. Nothing was left unaccounted for; we even created a "poop patrol" to be ready at the helm if nature called. Of course, Michele had the assistance of aunts and uncles in coordinating this event.

The morning of the "Photos with Santa" event, all six transport vehicles arrived. The first order of business was to dress all the pups in their Christmas best. Outfits were labeled and laid out days in advance. A master sheet indicated which transport vehicle would be transporting which dogs. (I explained the "science" behind pairing up dogs based on personalities, ailments, and so in chapter 9, "No Ordinary Day at the Beach.")

The Monkey's House caravan arrived at the mall and parked behind a vacant store so we could stage ourselves before the shoot. The Voorhees Animal Orphanage really went out of its way to make this happen for us. The staging area was adjacent to the place where the pictures were going to be taken. As we unloaded the cars, some dogs were put into wagons while others walked along the front of the store to reach the staging point. We had a mini-Monkey's House Christmas parade as they were all dressed in their holiday best.

Additional aunts and uncles arrived to help get the dogs organized, and then we waited for our turn to see Santa. As in previous years, the dogs were relaxed and enjoying the adventure. I don't recall any accidents, but if there were any, the poop patrol had it covered. Eventually, Monkey's House was called, and through a connecting door, we all strolled in and took our places. Once again, the volunteers who organized the event ensured we were lined up properly, and we ended up with a great picture. I think all the dogs got what they asked for from Santa that year.

With the growth of Monkey's House—the dogs that live at our house, those at forever fosters, and even a few "imposters" (they are always part of our family)—you can only imagine how challenging it is to get a venue that can accommodate all of us. Sadly, the Promenade informed us that they couldn't accommodate us any longer. Michele and I were so disappointed; the photos with Santa had turned into one of, if not *the*, pinnacle event of the year for us. Everybody loved this day, as did the many onlookers who took their four-legged family members to get pictures with Santa, too. At that moment, we thought there would be no pictures in 2018. We were crushed.

But as the saying goes, when one door closes another door opens, or maybe I should say, a "dog door opens," as thirty-five dogs went through that new door to a new venue, Redman's Garden Center. Redman's had heard of our predicament and welcomed us with open arms. They had a large stage set up outside with a beautiful tree and sleigh all fully decked out for the holidays. On that day we had the assistance of about twenty aunts and uncles, Santa Ray, and our friend Hugh, the photographer.

The game plan was pretty much the same as in previous years, but we had a few advantages this year over last. Although we didn't have Rudolph the Red-Nosed Reindeer leading the pack, we did one better: Waggin' One transported the pups to see Santa. What a convenience to be able to transport the family in one vehicle! Using Waggin' One ensures that no dogs get left behind.

Redman's allowed us to come an hour before the scheduled photos with Santa event. This was a huge benefit over previous years when we had to line up at the door ready to pounce into position next to Santa, snap the photo, then rush out to make room for the next "normal" family. Honestly, it was still quite hectic; we felt pressure to get out as quickly as possible; the line to see Santa was long with anxious dogs and pet parents.

As we rolled into Redman's parking lot, many of our forever fosters were waiting. "Everybody off the bus," I shouted. Once off the bus, the aunts and uncles made sure we didn't have any outfit malfunctions (pups, not humans). As I walked toward the stage, I noticed one of the other loves of my life, Betty, was already there. This imposter dog that had found her forever home with Vicki and Fred was standing nearby dressed in her holiday attire. It had been almost two years since I last saw Betty. I could see the love and gratitude in her eyes as I gave her a big hug. This chance encounter made a special day a spectacular day!

The Monkey's House's 2018 Christmas photo at Redmond's.
Photo courtesy of Hugh Mac Donald

For a while, our 2018 "Photos with Santa" looked like it would never take place. But I believe things do happen for a reason, and when your mission is honorable and heartfelt, others take notice and jump in to help when needed. The energy at this event was so different from previous years. Not being rushed, having a friend take the photos, and another friend play the role of Santa made all the difference in the world. There was a sense of calm and appreciation for the overall mission of Monkey's House, and this one occasion expressed it beautifully. There were dozens of group photos taken, and then each dog had its opportunity to shine with individual pictures on Santa's lap. Some dogs asked to have their special person included, while others, like Lucy and Mr. Peebody, wanted their picture taken together.

LUCY AND MR. PEEBODY

Lucy and Mr. Peebody love the "Photos with Santa" event, and it's not just getting the opportunity to sit on Santa's lap, begging him to deliver the smelliest cod skin treats straight from the North Pole on Christmas Eve. They love it all, from having their favorite aunts help them put on holiday attire only befitting proud beagles to taking a ride together in Waggin' One to being with all their furry friends, aunts and uncles, and finally to meeting Santa. This has to be the best day of the year for them, completely the opposite of their past lives of being part of a hunting pack. The sad truth is that aging is a death sentence for many hunting dogs. Lucy and Mr. Peebody's owner had no use for them any longer when they got older and dumped them at a kill shelter. Luckily, they made their way to us in 2015 when Monkey's House first opened.

Lucy and Mr. Peebody asking Santa for lots of presents.

The term *bonded pair* is thrown around a lot in the rescue world; shelters try to keep best friends together when possible and urge the pair be adopted by the same family. We had a few bonded pairs over the years. They all had a special connection but nothing like the connection between Lucy and Mr. Pee; they were truly inseparable. A loud snoring sound would always draw your attention toward Mr. Pee sleeping, but what really caught your eye was Lucy sleeping as close to him as possible. I would laugh as Lucy always had part of her body on top of Mr. Pee—a leg, her head—snuggled together like a typical sleeping couple. At times, you would see Mr. Pee squirming his body as if he were saying something like, "Move over, give me some room." Did somebody say dogs are a lot like their owners? Mr. Pee really did love Lucy. He slept with the biggest smile on his face when she was by his side.

When Lucy and Mr. Peebody first came to our farm, they lived in the barn. The thought of being in the house scared the heck out of

Sweet dreams, Lucy and Mr. Peebody.

them, which I quickly found out one day when I tried to bring them inside. Hunting beagles have outside pens with a small shelter. The transition to bringing them into the house took over a year. It took six months just to get them into the Cottage, which was their first step at getting acclimated to inside living. With all the comforts a home provides, they eventually thrived in that environment. At first, furniture was a new concept to them, but it didn't take long for them to have their favorite comfy spots. Gradually, they were transitioned into the house. You would never have known they were outside dogs except for one little issue. Mr. Pee was true to his name and was never fully housebroken, although he tried his best.

Walking the beagles is always a pleasure, but we quickly learned the walks had to be before 9 p.m. because Mr. Pee liked to sing on his walks. Depending on what animal scents were in the back field, he may end up singing the entire walk. His tenor didn't match that of the great singer Luciano Pavarotti, but his volume may have surpassed Luciano's! I'm sure the old farmhouse across the meadow heard Mr. Pee, and it wasn't any opera they would want to hear as they started to get ready for bed. Besides Lucy's sniffing sounds, she didn't make a peep, but boy was her tail going a mile a minute the entire walk.

That day at Redman's, I let Santa think I was his helper, his elf, but deep inside I grabbed the opportunity to be the alpha dog, if only in my own head. Like a ringmaster, I made sure all the dogs got up on Santa's lap or next to his feet, and ensured their best sides were highlighted in the photos. When I tossed Mr. Pee and Lucy on Santa's lap, I swore I heard Mr. Pee ask Santa for a bigger bed, and Lucy's head quickly turned to give him a look. During all of this, I noticed Michele standing on the corner of the stage taking it all in with tears in her eyes. I asked her if she were okay, and she replied, "Things couldn't be better. Each one of these dogs was slated to be destroyed. Instead, they're here and enjoying themselves sitting on Santa's lap."

Is Santa real? Do wishes come true?

I think the pups believe he is, and they do.

CHAPTER 13

THE BEST TEACHER IS A HOSPICE DOG

In my life, I've had many great teachers and coaches who taught me skills to navigate through life. With their guidance and my desire to learn, they molded me into the person I am today. Of course, seeking knowledge is never ending; it continues to shape our personalities and the paths we take to our last breaths. The key to gaining wisdom is to seek out the proper teacher. I find what makes life interesting is learning new things throughout the journey.

Around the time we started Monkey's House, I decided to become a teacher myself, a Yoga instructor. At that time, I had been practicing Yoga for about five years and loved both its physical and mental benefits. I had a solid Yoga practice and wanted to share these benefits with others. So, at the age of fifty five, I jumped in headfirst (literally, if you count headstands) to become the best instructor possible. Doing my research, I found a great program at a studio called Dig Yoga where I was trained by terrific instructors including Sue Elkind, Mariel Freeman, and Kilkenny Tremblay.

When most people think of Yoga, they think of the physical practice of performing poses in a sequence, called *asana*. However, Yoga is so much more. It's actually about achieving a balance among the mind, body, and soul. Any Yoga instructor will tell you that Yoga is practiced both on and off the mat; it's more of a way of living your life. With the pups at Monkey's House keeping me busy, I don't get to do the physical asana practice as much as I would like. When I tell my mentor Kilkenny that I'm not practicing Yoga, she'll contradict me and say, "Your mission is your Yoga." Yoga has helped me become grounded in our mission to save hospice dogs.

As much as I'm grateful for the teachers I've had over the years and the guidance they provided, none has matched the wisdom I've learned from the dogs of Monkey's House. Michele would agree wholeheartedly; she has said many times, "My nursing career prepared me for Monkey's House." Her medical background provided a tremendous base to build off of, expanding her understanding of dogs in virtually every aspect. We've both come away with extensive life lessons from living with and loving these dogs, but Michele has taken it much further; it's transformed her life totally. Through her hands-on experience, the amount of knowledge she's acquired ensures each and every dog that make its way to us is going to have the best chance at living the remainder of its life in comfort, be it strolling on the beach or sitting on Santa's lap.

BUCK—MICHELE'S GREATEST TEACHER

Out of all the dogs we've cared for, Michele's greatest teacher has been Buck. He was the third dog to make its way to Monkey's House shortly after we opened in the summer of 2015. We were struggling with how to define the concepts of *hospice, end stage, terminal,* and *dying.* We found that Buck met all of those criteria. He taught us more about fighting to live in his time here than we can begin to say. He taught us to believe in miracles and to keep hoping even when all hope is lost. He survived so many downward spirals. Michele has said,

"I was honored to be part of Buck's life and that he chose me to be his person. It was a God-send that he found his way to Monkey's House so early in our journey. He had much to teach

me—to teach all of us—about living, loving, and focusing on what body parts still work rather than on what parts don't. (Being) deaf, blind, (having a) bad heart, bad lungs, strokes, and a brain tumor didn't stop him from being an incredible teacher and friend."

Buck was part of the Three Puppeteers, which also included Daisy Mae and FiFi. These three were inseparable, and wherever their mom was they weren't far behind. In the evenings, Michele would take her spot on the sofa, then you would see those three all snuggle together as close to Michele as possible. Usually, one pup made its way into Michele's lap. Other pups were allowed on the sofa, but don't get too close to Michele, or they would pay the price from at least one of the Three Puppeteers! Buck was the last of the three remaining. As each of his pals passed, it was really hard to watch him grieve. When FiFi passed, his last partner in crime, he laid across Michele's lap and wouldn't let her leave him most of the day. Buck was with FiFi on her final day, all day. We're positive he was aware that she had become very sick and was now gone. Sometimes, we wonder if dogs have a better understanding of life and death then we realize. With the passing of his furry friends, his bond with Michele grew even stronger.

Buck celebrated four "gotcha days" with us. (A "gotcha day" is the annual anniversary of a dog's adoption or rescue.) Most of our hospice dogs get to see their first gotcha day, about 50 percent see their second, and we've had a handful make it to their third and fourth, like Buck. In our PBS video, Dr. Morgan was asked about the life span of our dogs.

"Some dogs that were given two weeks to live are still here a year later, doing good and are happy!" she answered.

We rejoiced at each and every gotcha day for Buck. He was a real living miracle. With excellent veterinary care, customized food therapy, and lots of love, he lived happily with a multitude of health issues and disabilities. He thrived here, overcoming health challenge after

Michele with FiFi and her boy Buck.

challenge. His second anniversary was celebrated with him in Michele's arms during a CNN taping for her *2017 CNN Hero* video. He is such a success story. His time here with us truly showed that although his body wasn't perfect, he had certainly brought companionship, joy, and love to all of us here at Monkey's House.

Before Monkey's House.

Buck was in very poor shape when he arrived at Monkey's House.

At Monkey's House.

Buck blossomed even with all his health issues.

Buck was going to be euthanized because he wasn't healthy. Sadly, that happens in shelters every single day across the country. Michele pointed out that had the shelter killed him, his death would not be counted against the shelter's "no-kill" statistics. A typical no-kill shelter's euthanasia policy reads something like: "we do not euthanize due to time or space constraints, reserving euthanasia for animals who are suffering mentally or physically, terminally ill, or considered dangerous." According to their policy it would have been acceptable to euthanize all of the dogs that eventually made their way to Monkey's House due to their terminal diagnosis. That's NOT acceptable to us!

Buck wasn't just eye candy; he was in fact Michele's navigator. On most of Michele's travels, she would have Buck and Sora with her. If Sora was the Zen master for the other dogs, then Buck was a calming presence for Michele. Michele would claim that Buck didn't like being without her and that he enjoyed car rides. This was all true, but I also think it was Michele's opportunity to give Buck a bit of extra attention. Michele said this about Buck:

> *"I would ask this blind, deaf copilot how to let my GPS know I want to take the option that will save five minutes. His answer was always the same: Pull over and figure it out yourself. On one occasion, coming from a veterinary appointment, I had my hand on Buck as he lay in his bed on the seat alongside me. His coat is silky, soft, and comfortingly familiar. I started wondering: How many dogs did he help me escort to appointments over the years. How many miles have we driven together? How much time have we spent together driving? This simple plan of bringing Buck along to add a little extra into his day over the years has brought so much joy, comfort, and peace into mine. Life is hectic; a bunch of short adventures can make up a lifetime. We need to remember to be mentally present for the ordinary stuff. Carly Simon was right, 'These are the good old days.'"*

We have a sofa swing in our backyard. Michele initially got it for the dogs to enjoy and hang out on. They were never really interested in it unless we are sitting on it. Now we're on it a lot with the pups. One evening after work the weather was great, so Michele and I took a few pups, and we all sat on the swing as the sun began to set. On that evening, Buck, Hannah Bear, and Fifi joined us.

"Déjà vu," Michele said. "Buck and I sat out here this morning. He sat right next to me alert and interested in the activity on the farm. I wondered what he was thinking, knowing he's deaf and blind. The wind started blowing the flowers off the cherry tree, and there was a bluebird inquisitively checking us out. I could see the Eastern Painted Turtle we named Cory floating on a log in the pond. I wondered if the wind brought more smells to Buck. Although my body was still, my mind was wandering. Buck just sat there, alert and content. Realizing he was just content to be hanging out together on a beautiful day, happy and peaceful, I decided to shut my mind off and just appreciate Buck, the bond I share with him. Dogs do so many things better than we do; being in the moment is hard, but it's wonderful. Appreciating the time we have with those we love, now that's one of the finest gifts we can give ourselves."

Michele's little companion lived vibrantly and loved fiercely for four years, three months, and three days. On Michele's *CNN Hero* interview, they used a quote that she lives by and surely did for Buck:

"It's very important to us that we don't fail them in their final moments. They have value, they deserve our love and dignity."

All the dogs that came through our doors have taught us the desire to overcome adversity, that love is all around us, and the value of living every moment to the fullest. Two recent pups that show us this joy for life are Dozer and Ariel. Both have major mobility issues and terminal diagnoses, but don't tell them that. They are some of the happiest dogs we've ever seen. They are on the opposite ends of the spectrum when it comes to size. Dozer is a ninety-pound German shepherd, Ariel is a Maltese-poodle mix weighing in just over four pounds. They both made their way to us just before the COVID-19 outbreak and have brought their own "new normal" to Monkey's House.

DOZER, A GENTLE GIANT

Apparently, they grow their dogs big in York, Pennsylvania. Dozer is the latest dog that we've taken from the York County SPCA. LA and Bullwinkle also came from their shelter. Besides large dogs, we have also received some of the friendliest dogs from their organization. The aunts and uncles, Michele and I will tell you it can be a real struggle helping these large dogs around as they lack mobility. I think we've all tweaked our backs on occasion, but if you ask any of us, we'll tell you it's worth every ache and pain caring and loving these gentle giants.

On Valentine's Day 2020, Michele and I decided to celebrate by giving our love to a special dog, Dozer. He has had quite a rough life and his people had let him down horribly, time and time again. He's paralyzed and has *degenerative myelopathy (DM)*. This is the canine

Dozer and Ariel took me for a walk on a nice spring day.

equivalent of *Amyotrophic Lateral Sclerosis (ALS)*, also known as *Lou Gehrig's disease*. We have had a few pups come through here with this diagnosis. The wonderful people at York County SPCA had been looking for a rescue placement for Dozer for quite a while. They had approached us about Dozer back in the fall when we didn't have the room. We had thought about and prayed for this pup for months until we were able to bring him here.

Our handsome Dozer needs a tremendous amount of time and attention, which we expected; however, his physical needs were more than we could handle with our normal setup (beds of all sizes, couches, etc.). We had been under the impression Dozer weighed seventy pounds and had the use of his front end. Well, he's ninety pounds with basically no use of his front legs; that makes a huge difference in his care. It was nearly impossible for any of us individually to move him. He needs his bladder expressed several times a day. That is a quick and easy thing to do, but in Dozer's case, he leaks constantly, not a problem that can be easily fixed with a belly band (belly bands are a wide strip of cloth with a disposable pad used for incontinent or "marking" male dogs.) His bedding needs to be changed and he needs to be cleaned and repositioned often. We knew there was a solution; we just needed to think outside the norm. After trying various options, we had a winner! Enter a gigantic landscape wagon. It's a beautiful addition for any family room, and it makes Dozer much more accessible. (I'm waiting to see it in the next Wayfair catalog. Maybe they can make a wood-grain model!)

The beauty of this wagon is that it sits a couple of feet off the ground, which saves our backs, knees, and sanity. The sanity part might be questionable; when I sit down to watch TV, I'm now looking right into Dozer's eyes! Being off the ground separates him from the other dogs, so he can safely enjoy bully sticks without most of the other pups knowing. Placed on the bed of the cart is a hospital-grade, alternating-pressure mattress to help with his very fragile skin, avoiding bed sores at all cost.

Great innovators like Benjamin Franklin or Thomas Edison would tell you that you first need to try and fail before you succeed. I can't say if Michele will be the next Steve Jobs, but she has learned from trying, failing, and eventually succeeding in bathing Dozer, keeping him clean and comfortable. She started with the antiquated bucket method, which then led to a livestock water tank, and eventually to the "Piney" swimming pool.

To quote Michele on the bucket method:

"This morning, I woke to a big pile of poo behind Dozer. It was on several parts of him, his bedding, on the tire, and the outside of the cart. Everywhere! For the record, there was none on the pee pad strategically placed to prevent this "storm." I'm bathing Dozer, the way I have been, all week. It's the way I have bathed large, immobile dogs for a while. I take the water pitcher, fill it with warm water, and just get to work. Aunt Claire walked in on 'the process' and was worried I had lost my mind. I guess from where she was standing, she saw me pouring water on Dozer as well as all over the floor; some would say I was working on an indoor pool. Next, Aunt Sandi came in, saw the disaster, and grabbed the dry vac and got right to work. I still thought things were under control and that I was doing a fantastic job helping Dozer to feel and smell better while trying to improve his skin. I'd be the first to admit I needed way more towels than usual, and there was a lot of water. In the middle of all of this, Aunt Terry walked in. She wasn't on the schedule, she just popped by. She saw what was going on. She could have turned and ran, but instead she chose to help. This speaks volumes to her integrity and character. Aunt Sandi was alternating between the dry vac and the mop. I'm still pouring water on Dozer; Claire is holding Dozer, and Terry jumps into action. They both get to work drying him. The story ends with Dozer on a clean, dry bed, and immaculate floors; what could possibly be wrong? There was a lot of giggling and a mountain of laundry. Every morning has a funny story, this one was a bit funnier than usual."

Learning from this near disaster, Michele went to the local farm store and purchased a low-livestock water tank that would accommodate Dozer's size. We started him on the *microbubble baths* to help maintain his good skin and hopefully heal some of his other skin issues and sores. It worked okay, but lifting Dozer into and out of the tank was still a problem. We do have a Hoyer lift that helps our backs, but it is still not an ideal setup.

A couple of days later, I went into the garage when Dozer was getting another bath. I noticed the stock tank was no longer being used. Michele had a heavy-duty tarp lining the inside of our smaller garden cart. She said this was her "Piney pool" method. ("Piney" is an endearing term used for folks that live in the Jersey Pine Barrens, and we do live in the Pines.) When she finished bathing Dozer, she rolled the cart outside with Dozer still soaking in the water, takes off the back panel, lowers the tarp, and voila, the water rushed out. Move over, Elon Musk!

Dozer loved his microbubble treatment.

Dozer loves his daily walks with his aunts and uncles. On one of the walks with his Aunt Marcia, as they were cruising down the road they met a gentleman in his car who had a lovely German shepherd named Rosie with him. He rolled down Rosie's window, the pups exchanged a few words in their native tongue, and just like that Dozer had a new friend named Rosie. On another occasion, Aunt Kristen took Dozer out to see the snow geese that gathered in the fields down the road. Snow geese are a sight to see—hundreds of white geese with black-tipped wings turning what was a brown field white because of their sheer numbers. Dover takes in the sights on his walks and is very attentive to his surroundings. When you make the turn to come home, he starts singing. We're not sure if he's excited to get home, wants to walk farther, or is singing for Rosie. (I was told Rosie was awful cute!)

Because of COVID-19 isolation rules, the pups are missing their favorite aunts and uncles. Working from home, I'm able to get out for a nice walk with Dozer at lunchtime. I'll generally grab our puppy, Carbon, to go along; I need to wear him out a little, if that's even possible! Dozer has a separate cart that we use for baths and walking. It's slightly smaller than the one in the family room, and he uses it to get around in the house. We just pull it up to his bigger chart and load him up. While I'm out walking, it gives Michele time to get his bed all cleaned up. Many times, after his walk, he'll get his bath.

Dozer has joined the other pups at PetPT starting underwater treadmill exercises (much like LA does, Dozer has a veterinary technician in the water behind him moving his back legs to the rhythm of his front legs), cold laser, and acupuncture treatments. Dr. Howe-Smith and Aunt Beth got Dozer into a quad cart that was put together from parts of other carts; the front legs and wheels had belonged to our Holly. (It brought back bittersweet memories of Holly. Her story is coming up in chapter 14, "The Journey Forward.") The cart allows Dozer a moment of normalcy in a world in which he has no control.

ARIEL, "LION OF GOD"

After Michele went through her trial and errors in getting Dozer organized, she didn't have quite the same issues with Ariel, weighing in at less than five pounds. The name Ariel means "lion of God" in Hebrew, and since she's a force to be reckoned with, it seems to fit. (Thanks to Liz from Liz's Rescue Wagon for this name for our sweet little girl that surely needed Monkey's House.)

This little pup suffered immensely because of owner neglect. Ariel only has her two front legs; she chewed off one of her back legs. It was broken and the pain was too much for her to bear. The other back leg is missing the lower third; we don't know the story behind that one. When Ariel was rescued, these missing appendages weren't obvious because she was so badly matted. She also has cancer in the form of mammary masses and isn't spayed. Ariel is very thin with little muscle mass. We saw tremendous improvement in just a few short weeks. She is feeling a lot better now, loved beyond measure, pampered, and will be adored until her final breath.

Ariel visited Aunt Sandie from Di-Oh-Geez Grooming for a makeover. Aunt Sandi and her team always do such a nice job on the Monkey's House pups; their beautification of Ariel was no exception, and she smelled great, too.

Michele took Ariel to PetPT to get fitted for a cart. With a few adjustments, Dr. Howe-Smith quickly worked his magic. Suddenly, she started walking around and then went flying out of the room and down the hall. Everyone was cheering her on with happy tears in their eyes. While racing down the hall, our new pup ran right into Dr. Knight who was on her way over to examine Ariel and was beyond thrilled to encounter our little speed demon.

After feeding all the dogs, we get them ready to go out for walks; the first to get organized is Ariel. Michele gets her in her little cart and off she goes. No leash; she adores Michele and won't stray far. For all the trips Michele takes up and down the driveway, into the front yard, or around the back field, Ariel is right there. She speeds up significantly for chickens, cats, rabbits, and our poor delivery person.

Ariel is tuckered out from playing with all the other dogs.

She's living life, enjoying the freedom the wheels provide her, never giving a second thought to her missing back legs.

We are thrilled to have the privilege to show Ariel the other side of the human race; even our pups are excited to have her here. Ariel has quickly made friends with our puppy, Carbon. They have become great play buddies, and although she's as rough as can be, he's extremely gentle with her.

When life dealt Dozer and Ariel lemons, not only did they make lemonade but they also set up a stand and gave it away free along with life lessons we can learn through their actions. These two very special pups inspire me every day; they've taught me that nothing can keep the spirit down. *Life can come crashing down on you like a ton of bricks. You have to get up, dust yourself off, and find a way to keep living.* That's what our pups do every day.

Most of us have challenges today or have had one or more in the past. It's safe to say we'll all experience them in our lifetimes; honestly, they are part of life. You—no one—can escape them. How you handle your particular situation is what matters. Hospice dogs can teach us so much. They live in the moment, enjoying those little things that we don't even notice. They don't let a terminal illness stop their living, and neither should we. Our dogs have taught us some great lessons:

- With the right amount of passion, you can make the world a better place. Monkey helped us discover ours and start Monkey's House.

- When you find something you like, keep doing it (or eating it, as MLBob did with his peanut butter pies).

- If you don't like your attitude, change your environment. Shark came here angry and full of skepticism; today, he's happy and trusting.

- We all can be a positive influence on a child. It didn't take Bugsy long to get Kaiden to sleep through the night in his own bed.

- Even when things look bleak, you'll always find your way back home. Matt did.

- Be open; it only takes a moment to fall in love. Bo stole our hearts the instant we looked into his eyes.

- Go out and conquer the world! Melvin did, if only in his mind.

- Don't let your limitations stop you from enjoying today. Tequilla would love to join you for a stroll on the beach.

- Find that special Lucy or Mr. Peebody in your life and love her or him like there's no tomorrow.

- There is nothing better than fresh air and sun on your face when you're feeling gloomy. LA would guarantee it.

- Not every approach will fix your problems; keep trying until you find one that works for you. Cotton hated acupuncture but loved cold laser therapy.

- We all have something to offer until our final breaths. You may even save a life like Pete did.
- Don't take life too seriously. Hooch recommended surfing and snacking on bananas.

Through Monkey's House, we hope to show the world by example, education, and inspiration that hospice dogs have a lot to offer. We love to hear about the positive influences we've had on our global family. We absolutely love it when we hear, "In following Monkey's House, you've given us the courage and knowledge to adopt a senior dog with special needs." Those are the best words we can ever hear! We received a great note from Ginny who said the following:

> *"I just wanted to let you know how much you taught me over the past year. I've scoured your posts for hope and help as I struggled to keep Bella going comfortably. You showed me how to be patient during setbacks and how to cherish each small moment. As Bella's limitations mounted, I agonized over her quality of life and always looked to you for guidance. When you said, "There's always a chance for a better tomorrow," I felt so comforted. And so many times there were better tomorrows. Thank you for the inspiration you gave me."*

I pray that someday when I'm in my final chapter, I remember the lessons the dogs of Monkey's House have taught me, and LIVE to my final breath.

CHAPTER 14

THE JOURNEY FORWARD

New Year's Day for us isn't about making up simple resolutions that we all find ourselves breaking within a few days or weeks. It's an opportunity to pause and look back and celebrate all the dogs that have come and gone through the past year. It's a time to be thankful for the opportunity to have gotten to know them, be a part of their lives, and give them the best final chapter possible. We don't reflect on the sad moments; we relish in the victories no matter how small they might be. We delight in the happy and sometimes funny moments that we all helped make possible. We remind ourselves of what makes us who we are and of what we need to keep doing to save and care for these once-homeless hospice dogs that deserve a better ending.

We love being with our pack of furry friends and aunts and uncles alike, effortlessly living in the moment, no big gestures yet so many small ones that are meaningful for us all. On this special day, we gather up all the dogs, load them into Waggin' One, and head to Brendan T. Byrne State Forest, one of our special hideaways located in the heart of the New Jersey Pine Barrens. This is a lesser-known park in a state that's the most populist in the country for its size. The Pine Barrens is one of *the* greatest "undiscovered" wonders of New Jersey, and we would like to keep it that way. The other beauty of this park is its location, just ten minutes from our house.

On New Year's Day in New Jersey, you never can tell what the weather will be like. Luckily, we have a few hiking options, and we'll make the final decision on the morning of the hike. On a mild sunny day, we might opt for a hike around the old cranberry bogs and get to witness the majestic beauty of the tundra swans. The dogs, aunts and uncles are in awe of them; hearing their bugling calls and seeing them take flight are quite an experience. If the weather is just right, the sightseeing swan option is always a winner.

On the opposite end of the spectrum, if it's a cold, windy day, we'll opt for a trail nestled among the tall pines and oaks to give us cover from the howling winds. It's an extrawide ADA (American with Disabilities Act) trail that can accommodate a wheelchair, thus a great choice for us with our strollers and wagons.

The in-between option is a trip to Pakim Pond. At the trail head is a pretty pond with a few gazebos and picnic tables. You get the best of both worlds with some open water and protected trails.

On this occasion, as I pulled Waggin' One into the parking lot of Pakim Pond, to our surprise the parking lot was almost full. Seems word got out about our annual tradition and others are adopting it and celebrating the New Year here, too—just not as many folks being led by dogs! The unloading of the wagon, strollers, and then of course the dogs is like clockwork (well, maybe with a broken second hand). The unloading process always seems to be a little more hectic than the loading process as everybody is excited to start the adventure. Once unloaded, we get an onlooker to snap a few group photos, and off we go past Pakim Pond and onto the trail.

Much like our beach trip, the time on the trail is limited because a majority of the dogs have reduced physical abilities. The keys here are to get the dogs into the fresh air, let them see some new sights, and experience different smells. Mostly we are out to have a good time. I like to think our outing on the first day of the year keeps true to Monkey's House's journey and sets the tone for the coming year.

HOLLY, A LOVELY SOUL WITH THE LONGEST JOURNEY

People are always saying they don't know how we can do this day in and day out. There is no magic pill, there is no "professional distance," and there are no tricks. We willingly give up our hearts to be crushed time and time again. But there is another side to what we do, something so incredibly beautiful, mysterious, honest, and pure. We lead these dogs on a new and final journey full of love and dignity.

Out of all the dogs we have taken in, it's hard to say which might have had the longest journey—not in time spent at Monkey's House, but in terms of their transformational journey— after taking that first step into Monkey's House, but Holly certainly would be one. She came here in November of 2016. I remember Michele saying, "She's the thinnest dog I have ever seen"; after many months, Michele added to that statement, "that lived." Michele was not sure Holly would make it; emaciated would not even describe this German shepherd mix weighing in at twenty-seven pounds. Michele was right; she was by far the thinnest dog we had taken in. She was quiet and lifeless at first, then the growling started—at everyone. It was hard to blame her with the way she had been previously treated. Our job was to show her the kinder side of humanity.

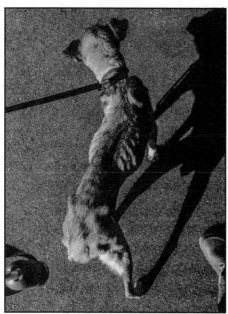

The day Holly arrived at Monkey's House.

The first six weeks Holly spent at Monkey's House, Michele was the only person she permitted to get her out of her suite. She would rather look at a wall than at people until she learned people carried treats and shared them if she looked their way. As she improved, she made it clear she wasn't comfortable with other animals. We called in one of the dog trainers we work with to consult about Holly's demeanor, getting some guidance on the next steps. We took her on daily walks to get her acclimated to the farm. Joining us on this jaunt around the property was our cat Grandpa, Holly's first companion here.

Once Holly became more settled, the pack walks started, day in and day out, for weeks. With the progression of the pack walks, one of the rooms in the Cottage was divided in half, which allowed Holly to be "with" three quiet, even-tempered dogs, yet separated by an x-pen (an x-pen is much like a plan pen for a young child to keep them safe and out of trouble.) This gave Holly the opportunity to watch and learn how the other dogs interacted. We had "supervised times" where Holly hung out in the yard with the other dogs. Then one day Holly was ready. The transition from living alone to living with her own little family was completed; she was living peacefully and happily with the other pups in the Cottage. She amazed and astounded us more times than we could say, progressing from growling at everybody to loving people, cats, and even "tolerating" other dogs.

Holly was a changed dog, enjoying life. Laying out in the sun and taking short walks were some of her favorite pastimes. On many occasions, as she lay outside enjoying the sun in her face, Grandpa would curl up alongside her, or should I say, more on top of her! Over time, she enjoyed the company of the other dogs, too, giving comfort to Maggie as she neared the end of her life. Maggie was not one of the original Cottage crew, but she was having issues getting in and out of the main house because of the steps. Since there were no steps in the Cottage, we moved her there. Besides improving Maggie's mobility, a friendship blossomed with Holly; it was an incredibly beautiful and unexpected occurrence. Dying sounds like such a sad, final venture, but if you can be open to living even while experiencing the dying process, it can be beautiful, filled with friends and love, like the love Holly gave to Maggie.

Holly and her good friend Maggie.

We always suspected Holly had *degenerative myelopathy (DM)*, the doggy version of *Amyotrophic Lateral Sclerosis (ALS)* that Dozer had. Her ability to get around was deteriorating as time went on. We tried many options, and since we've seen good results with water therapy, we decided to start Holly on that regimen. She really enjoyed those days. I'm not sure if it were the underwater treadmill workout or the rides home, because for some reason Aunt Trudy's GPS would detour them to an Arby's almost every time!

Dr. Howe-Smith later diagnosed Holly with a spinal tumor. Eventually, Holly needed a quad cart to get around. Luckily, we had a donated cart that fit her well with just a few minor adjustments. I thought of the cart not as a symbol of disability but as a chariot of independence. The cart gave Holly the freedom and dignity we would all want if we were in her circumstance.

Unfortunately, over time Holly lost the use of her back legs. The good news was that any pain she might have been experiencing was gone; she was pain-free. She was eating up a storm, and there was a Zen aura about her in her new routine. She would get bathed daily; protecting skin from the perils of incontinence and immobility is a very high priority. We offered her water frequently and turned her from side to side multiple times a day. It was necessary to hold her up to drain her bladder. We would also put a sling under her hind end so she could walk a bit. She was happy, even content it seemed. Her soft brown eyes were filled with trust and peace. Like always, it was our time to show her our love and commitment to her was truly unconditional.

It was a beautiful, sunny day when Holly made her journey to the Rainbow Bridge. It was a great day to lay in the sun for a bit, then head off to heaven. It was Holly's plan, we just didn't know it; she planned it out perfectly all by herself. The sofa was arranged in the Cottage to catch the best breeze and still feel the sunshine. She was hand-fed breakfast by Aunt Claire, and when the time came, she was surrounded by aunts and uncles to see her off to heaven. Holly made a remarkable transformation in fifteen months. We are incredibly honored to have been part of such a lovely soul's life.

Michele has pointed out many times that dogs get pleasure in small things, and they're not just good but as she puts it, "they're amazing." Caring for the dogs can surely wear you down at times, but with a pat on a furry head and the look in their eyes, we can all experience those little pleasures, too.

Holly became one of my favorite dogs; I saw the gratitude in her eyes. She eventually trusted us with all aspects of her life. For a period of time, it was really hard to get Holly to eat; she was a "licker," a dog that licks its food out of the bowl instead of eating it. As you can imagine, a licker takes a long time to eat, which is not good for a dog with stomach issues. Holly would generally stop eating without much getting down the hatch. I started to hand-feed her; after scooping up some food, Holly would eat it right out of my hand, actually gulping it at times. I could get her to eat much faster that way, and generally she would eat the entire meal, pills and all.

When I first started this routine, I have to admit it was a little nasty, but it quickly turned into one of my little pleasures. It's hard to describe why; all I can say is Holly was eating and we got to spend some quality time together. There was one issue with this method, though; she often mistakenly and gently bit my finger or hand. I would jokingly tell Holly that was not food; it was our running joke. Finally, I'd feel her tongue getting the final scraps off my hand. It was a very rewarding time of my evening. It wasn't just good, it *was* amazing!

PRINCESS GRANNY, TRUE ROYALTY

What would you think if I told you about a senior dog that had trouble walking, a heart murmur, severe dental disease, was deaf, blind, and terrified? Would you wonder how a dog in this condition could start over? What kind of life would it lead? Would it be a life of quality?

These are all legitimate questions; what we can tell you is that they deserve a chance. Granny got just that chance as she made her way to Monkey's House with the help from a few friends. Her name was quickly changed to Princess Granny. Her mobility issues were addressed and fixed and disabling mats of hair removed. She spent her time in quarantine foster with Aunt Denise. Denise's daughter said it best: "Princess Granny's breath smells like three-hundred dead hermit crabs." She was right; bad breath is a telltale sign of dental disease, and Princess Granny's was bad.

Princess Granny was a puppy mill momma who by our estimates made tens of thousands of dollars for her owner producing scores of Pekingese litters. It wasn't until she was old, blind, hard of hearing, severely matted, and developed significant heart problems that she was thrown away, ending up at a kill shelter. That was before. After we rescued her, Aunt Denise pampered her; she had favorite foods, clothes to keep her old body warm, and extra soft blankets. When Michele picked her up to bring her here, she came with a Nordstrom's bag full of her own things. In just two weeks, Princess Granny went from a matted, spinning, homeless dog to a sweet pup who now has a fully accessorized stylish wardrobe, improving health, and a caring network of folks to look out for her—because she finally mattered.

Princess Granny didn't fall in love with us right away, but she did fall head over heels for her Aunt Karen. Every weekend like clockwork, Aunt Karen comes to do one of the morning feedings and spends half her day caring and cuddling the pups. Her favorite of course was Princess Granny. Like any true princess, Princess Granny had to have a tiara; actually, she had five in varying colors to match any outfit she might be wearing that day. On one occasion, I caught Karen wearing a matching tiara! Princess Granny could be moody, even to Aunt Karen, but it was taken in stride. Aunt Karen would start scratching her belly; it must have been ecstasy for Princess Granny. This would put her into a backbend in Karen's arms with her head reaching for the floor.

Aunt Karen's words on Princess Granny:

"They say that people have 'a type,' a set of physical attributes that they are innately and unconsciously drawn toward. When it comes to dogs, I love them all but I am drawn to the 'fluffy' ones preferably with a 'smooshed' face. Having grown up with a black Labrador, I had no experience with small dogs. I came to rescue a shih tzu mix in 2010 and a large part of my heart was forever changed. Fast forward to the summer of 2017, I came across a video on Facebook about a couple (Michele and Jeff Allen) and a bunch of volunteers who were caring for hospice dogs. I had never heard of such a thing and I was intrigued by a fluffy orange Pomeranian who was a resident there, his name was Pumpkin. I started digging into the place called Monkey's House and their mission. I fell more in love with the dogs and the people and decided I needed to volunteer there even though it was about an hour from my house. Before I was able to start volunteering, Pumpkin passed away. I was so very sad even though I had never met him.

On my first day of orientation, Monkey's House was everything I dreamed of and more. The dogs, Michele and Jeff, the other volunteers, and the space are truly amazing and well worth the drive. On that day, a new pup had joined the house that captured my attention, Princess Granny. She was a beautiful orange, fluffy, smooshed-face ball of fire and energy who loved to wear a crown. I was captivated. Princess Granny had such a bold character I was drawn to her even though she was not impressed with me. As a matter of fact, she wasn't impressed with anyone so I didn't really take it personally. Because Princess Granny was a bit more challenging, I used a slower approach with her than (I did with) the friendlier dogs. After a few visits and a lot of patience, I was able to handle Princess Granny. I had a specific method of touching her before I would pick her up; it was kind of like our secret handshake. I really enjoyed holding Granny and petting her, on her terms of course. Eventually I found a secret spot on Granny's chest that when scratched just the right way, would cause her to melt like a stick of butter in the sun. This became my goal every time I went to Monkey's House and always caused a laughing good time for us.

Anytime a Monkey's House outing was organized, I looked forward to pushing Granny in the Dogger. We went on so many journeys together. Granny enjoyed those adventures, and I know the time we spent together contributed to making her time at Monkey's House the best time of her life, as we call them, 'their best last days.'

During one of my days at Monkey's House, I gave the Princess a bath, or a 'royal bath' as we would call it. Since it was a nice day, I decided to sit on the deck in the sun to dry the Princess. While I was drying her belly, I noticed what I thought was a se- ries of weird freckles. I realized the 'freckles' were actually very poorly tattooed numbers; I was shocked and mortified! Dogs are tattooed for two reasons, for experimentation or they are a breeder dog. As if I weren't horrified enough by the tattooing of a dog, I was now even more horrified to imagine the pain and trauma Princess Granny was forced to endure in her life. Her life prior to Monkey's House caused her to not trust humans. I didn't really care about Granny's past; I wanted to be part of making her future as wonderful as possible. I would like to think that I helped her trust people and maybe even like us.

When Princess Granny's time to leave us arrived, I was honored to be the person to hold her as she exited her body and crossed the Rainbow Bridge. While I was holding Princess Granny and sobbing the gut-wrenching sobs brought on by the loss of a loved one, the veterinarian made a comment that I have held with me to this day. She remarked how wonderful it was that Princess Granny had gone from being an unwanted shelter dog to having a person who loved her so much that she was sobbing over her passing. Princess Granny taught me many lessons about life, resilience, standing up for yourself, forgiveness, and standing tall with a crown on your head."

Princess Granny and Sir Cotton out for a ride around the pond.

Princess Granny and her Aunt Karen.

Princess Granny participated in just about every trip we've taken. Wherever Princess Granny went, so did the Dogger dog stroller, also known as her royal carriage. Instead of horses pulling a princess, it was generally her Aunt Karen pushing her on the Jersey Shore or in the New Jersey Pine Barrens. A little over a year after Princess Granny came to Monkey's House, a dapper male Pekingese arrived, Cotton. Aunt Karen nicknamed him Sir Cotton, and the two of them traveled everywhere in their royal carriage together.

There is always such commotion around the British royal family; it was no different with Princess Granny. She was loved by all her followers and was treated like the true royalty she was for over two years. She made her way to the castle past the Rainbow Bridge on her loving servant's lap, Aunt Karen, wearing her tiara. We're sure she met up with Sir Cotton and is traveling in style in her royal carriage.

SWEET VIOLET

A "freedom ride" is the start of a new journey for a dog; for hospice dogs, it is lifesaving. It entails giving up one's afternoon and going to a shelter to pick up the smelliest dog that may well have active fleas or kennel cough. During the ride back to Monkey's House, the dog might urinate, defecate, or even vomit in your car. With the price of gas, the cost of maintaining cars, and considering the most important factor, your precious time, why would anyone do this? The ear-to-ear smile on Aunt Dawn's face when she arrived at Monkey's House with Trouble (that was her name, really) is why.

Cars air out and messes get cleaned up. To be the one on the other end of the leash as a dog walks out of the shelter is an incredible and awe-inspiring moment. Those of us in the dog rescue business work hard to help dogs beat the odds, and we relish every single second of a "freedom ride."

We agreed that Trouble was a name that did not suit her at all; this black Lab mix deserved a name befitting a beautiful soul. We agreed on Violet. She was a bit frightened in her new environment, and as Michele's grandmother would say, "She's a mell of a hess."

Besides the normal dental work that most of our seniors need when they arrive, Violet also had a very large tumor that was right between her eyes. It was the size of a large fist that would flop from side to side as she walked, totally covering one eye while pulling on the other. To make matters worse, it was ulcerated and infected. It was difficult to watch her drink or eat as the tumor would fall right into her bowl. Aunt Dawn called it her "portabella mushroom."

Violet with the nasty tumor
between her eyes.

We didn't have a quarantine foster available for Violet, so we kept her in our barn. We've temporarily kept dogs there before and had installed a large fenced-in area allowing them to get some fresh air and sun. Luckily, we didn't drop our quarantine standards and say, "Oh well, let's just put her in one of the suites in the garage," as she developed an extreme case of kennel cough. If anybody saw us going out to care for her, they might have thought they were watching a sci-fi movie. Halfway to the barn is a little shed where we had surgical gowns, booties, and gloves. If we had any contact with Violet, we had to be covered neck to toes. Once out of her area, the protective personal equipment (PPE) came right off and was immediately tossed into a trash bag.

Aunt Trish and Aunt Sandie devised a way for sweet Violet to get a great, anti-itch bath in her quarantine area. She loved the attention. The more time you spent with her, the more head over heels you would be for her. Three weeks seemed like an eternity, but she got over the cough and was ready to *live*.

Top on the agenda was to remove that mushroom from between her eyes. Violet sailed through surgery; however, we were a little blindsided by the news that her jaw was previously broken and had healed incorrectly. She had a pocket in her mouth that hid a group of teeth that were removed without extraction; they were just scooped out. Dr. Morgan once again did a wonderful procedure. Michele is often in the operating room during surgical procedures, lending a hand or just gaining knowledge. She was there for Violet's surgery and said the one thing Dr. Morgan didn't have was the music you often hear playing during operations on TV shows. Michele said she should have been playing Roberta Flack's, "The First Time Ever I Saw Your Face."

When one's life is heavily impacted by physical and emotional pain, who you become is a factor of those who reached out to you during those painful times in your life. We've been blessed to learn kindness and compassion from two- and four-legged beings. We don't know who was there for Violet; we fear no one. Yet she is sweeter and kinder than we could ever describe or aspire to be. Her biopsy came back as basal cell carcinoma, but fortunately that cancer has never spread.

Violet and I have become great hiking buddies, journeying down more paths in the state forest than I can count. She loves to walk, not stroll mind you, but at a "let's go" pace! It is quite different from walking with the other Monkey's House's seniors. I cherished my time with Violet, yet sadness was setting in. I knew her path was not with me in the Pines; she needed her own family. As I looked into those beautiful brown eyes, I could tell Violet was an imposter.

We thought Violet had hit the lottery as we sent her to a foster of Tiny Paws Rescue where she would polish her skill of living in a home without twenty-plus brothers and sisters and be adopted into a loving family. Not all fosters work out, and Violet found her way back to Monkey's House after a few months. This was a sad moment for us; we had been hopeful she would find her own family.

Apparently though, Violet was right where she was meant to be, at Monkey's House. She developed a very aggressive form of mouth cancer shortly after returning to us. It was a different type of cancer from the mass she previously had on her face. The diagnosis was not good, and we were advised that part of her lower jaw and tongue need- ed to be removed, followed by chemo and radiation. We didn't think she could have a good quality of life if she had that procedure and felt that was no way to live out her final months, so we sought alternatives in nontraditional medicine and chose *neoplasene treatment*. *Neoplasene* is derived from *bloodroot*, an old herb used by Native Americans. It's generally applied in a salve that is rubbed on the tumor, in pill form, or injected in the vein or around the tumor. This treatment will reduce the size of the tumor by killing cancer cells while it stimulates the immune system.

After the procedure, her mouth might be a little sore over the next few days, but Dr. Morgan prescribed something to keep her comfy. She will be good to go until the mass starts to return again. We were so grateful for this alternative treatment modality. Violet is truly a walking miracle. Living well with cancer is sometimes the best life that can be attained. Violet is also on a very low carb diet, which is known to slow the growth of cancer.

Did I say I got my hiking buddy back? It's like we didn't miss a step! Violet and I go out to the park whenever possible, except on Sundays. That day is reserved for her favorite aunt, Aunt Marcia, to enjoy a walk and spend quality time together. Violet has a very fast strut; with each step, her front shoulder dips, making her ears flop like the wings of a dove. Violet doesn't know her time is limited, and we don't know how long she has, but I can tell you a year has come and gone since her diagnosis, and there's no sign of Violet slowing down.

Heading back from the park one day, we took a different route and the long way home, a scenic drive to do a little sightseeing. Violet gave me a glance like, "Where are we going, are we lost?"

I told her, "We're not lost. Let's savor the time we have together. We'll celebrate this moment—the gift of borrowed time. Look around, there's beauty on this journey. Although we'll struggle at times, the view on this ride will be treasured forever."

Over a hundred lucky dogs have made our home part of their journey, their "long way home." Their journeys are not always easy, but they celebrate life and make special moments count. With Monkey's House's motto, "WHERE DOGS GO TO LIVE," I can only imagine the stories they take to the Rainbow Bridge.

A happy Violet on her ride home from the park.

CONCLUSION
"LIVE YOUR DASH"

I'll never forget that magical day in 2018 when we took the pups to meet Santa on our annual "Photos with Santa" trip. At one point, I looked over and noticed tears running down Michele's cheek. When I asked her what was wrong, she replied, "Nothing; everything is just right. All of these dogs were lost souls waiting to be euthanized, and now they're sitting on Santa's lap asking for goodies as they get their picture taken. Nothing could be better."

When we started Monkey's House in 2015, we never dreamed we would have saved and cared for over a hundred once-homeless hospice dogs. Not only were they no longer homeless but they were also being given dignity and love—a second chance at living—and they relished all of it as did we. Nor did we realize that tens of thousands of people on social media would be loving these dogs from around the globe.

Our favorite poem is "The Dash" by Linda Ellis. For those who aren't familiar with this poem, we suggest you not only read it but also live it. In a nutshell: Your gravestone will be engraved with your birth date and the day you pass, separated by a dash. What matters in your life is not those dates but the *dash*, that is, how you *lived your life*. We feel the same about each dog of Monkey's House. We don't know that much if anything about their previous lives let alone their birth dates, and we don't think of their end dates. Our mission is to make their "dashes" the best they can be!

Over the years, we have been honored to share the dashes of all of the dogs: Fletcher, the German shepherd that befriended a little boy named Kaiden, giving him friendship and confidence; Bea, in spite of a broken body, going on picnics with her favorite Aunt Tracey; Tequilla, the handsome cocker with no eyes but that still had the day of his life at the Jersey Shore; Hannah Bear, notwithstanding a body full of cancer, did not slow down as her favorite pastimes were chasing cats and sitting on laps; Pete, a search and rescue dog, found a neighbor in need, making his last save; Violet, strutting her stuff and exploring new paths in the Pine Barrens as I struggle to keep up; Buck, managing to fool the experts by living longer than anyone expected, over four years, and one of Michele's greatest teachers. And of course, there was that little guy that started it all, Monkey, the little Heinz-57 pup that we fell head over heels for and in his name started Monkey's House.

"Live your dash" by helping others live theirs. There is no greater reward than saving a life or making someone else's life better. We all have the ability to volunteer, donate, start a nonprofit, or be a voice for a cause—spread the word. We can all make miracles happen!

THANKS FOR READING
WHERE DOGS GO TO LIVE!

NOW IS THE TIME TO TAKE ACTION!

- If you enjoyed this book, please consider leaving an honest review on the book's product page at the online bookstore where you purchased it. I will read them all. Thank you.

- Recommend this book to your dog-loving friends and family. Give a big shout-out on your social media platform.

- Support/volunteer at Monkey's House; we have many ways you can help outlined on our website: www.monkeyshouse.org

- Become part of the Monkey's House family, follow the pups on:
    - Facebook: www.facebook.com/monkeyshouse.org
    - Instagram: www.instagram.com/monkeyshouse_doghospice

- Book Jeff or Michele to speak at your upcoming event. Contact us via www.monkeyshouse.org

Jeff taking action, getting LA down to the beach to be with her pack.

RESOURCES

The following resources are mentioned in the book and/or are used by Monkey's House to improve the lives of our residents. Other sites have been listed that we found to be a great source of information to help you maintain or improve your dog's health so that they can enjoy their life and remaining years to the fullest extent possible.

VETERINARIANS/PHYSICAL THERAPISTS

Dr. Sarah Ball-Garino (www.gardenstateanimalhospital.com)

Dr. Brad Bates** (www.lapoflove.com)

Dr. Karen Becker (www.drkarenbecker.com)

Dr. Peter Dobias (www.peterdobias.com)

Dr. Russell Howe-Smith* (https://www.facebook.com/PetPT)

Dr. Noelle Knight* (https://www.facebook.com/PetPT)

Dr. Michael Miller* Cardiologist (www.gardenstateanimalhospital.com)

Dr. Judy Morgan* (www.drjudymorgan.com)

Dr. Shelby L. Reinstein* Ophthalmologist (www.vsecvet.com)

HousePaws** (www.housepaws.us)

Sarah MacKeigan PT (www.upwarddogrehab.com)

Sally Morgan PT (www.sallymorganpt.com)

Beth Tomasello CCRS (https://www.facebook.com/PetPT)

*Monkey's House Veterinarians
**In-home Euthanasia Services

FOOD AND SUPPLEMENTS

Allprovide (www.allprovide.com)—Manufacturers and suppliers of premium quality, natural dog and cat foods.

Adored Beast Apothecary (www.adoredbeast.com)

AminAvast Renal Support (www.aminavast.com)

CBD Dog Health (www.cbddoghealth.com)

Cocotherapy (www.cocotherapy.com)

Dr. Becker's Bites (www.drbeckersbites.com)

Dr. Dobias Natural Healing (www.peterdobias.com)

Dr. Harvey's (www.drharveys.com)

Dr. Mercola (https://healthypets.mercola.com)

Naturally Healthy Pets (www.drjudymorgan.com)

Rx Vitamins (www.rxvitamins.com)

GROOMING

Di-Oh-Geez Grooming by Aunt Sandie (https://groomingbyauntsandie.business.site)

Floss's Grooming (www.flossgrooming.com)

kin+kind (www.kin-kind.com)—All-natural, pet-grooming products

MOBILITY AIDS

The Dogger (www.dogquality.com/collections/dog-strollers) —The SUV of dog strollers

Dr. Buzby's ToeGrips® (www.toegrips.com) —Instant traction for senior and special-needs dogs who struggle to walk on slippery floors

Eddie's Wheels (www.eddieswheels.com)—Dog wheelchairs

Help 'Em Up Harness (www.helpemup.com) —A full-body, dog mobility harness

K9 Sport Sack (www.k9sportsack.com) —Forward-facing backpack dog carrier

Ruffwear (www.ruffwear.com)—Dog harnesses

RESCUE ORGANIZATIONS

Brookline Labrador Retriever Rescue (www.brooklinelabrescue.org)

Happy Tails Rescue Retirement Home
(www.happytailsrescueretirementhome.com)

Hart-2-Heart Rescue (www.facebook.com/Hart2HeartRescue)

Humane Society of Missouri-Shelter Buddies Reading Program
(www.hsmo.org/shelterbuddies)

J & Co. Rescue (www.jandcorescue.weebly.com)

Liz's Rescue Wagon (www.facebook.com/lizsrescuewagon)

Monkey's House a Dog Hospice & Sanctuary
(www.monkeyshouse.org)

Muttville Senior Dog Rescue (www.muttville.org)

NJ Aid for Animals (www.njafa.org)

Old Dog Haven (www.olddoghaven.org)

One Love Animal Rescue (www.oneloveanimalrescue.org)

Schultz Senior Dachshund Rescue/Sanctuary
(www.schultzseniordachshundsanctuary.weebly.com)

South Jersey Regional Animal Shelter
(www.southjerseyregionalanimalshelter.org)

Tiny Paws Rescue (www.tprescue.org)

Voorhees Animal Orphanage (www.vaonj.org)

York County SPCA (www.ycspca.org)

DOG BOOKS

Coffey, Laura T (www.myolddogbook.com), *My Old Dog*. Novato,
CA: New World Library, September 29, 2015

Morgan, Dr. Judy, *From Needles to Natural*. Blooming, IN: Archway
Publishing, July 15, 2014

Morgan, Dr. Judy, and Hue Grant, *Yin & Yang Nutrition for Dogs*.
USA: Thirty Six Paws Press, November 30, 2017

Rosenfelt, David (www.davidrosenfelt.com), *Dogtripping*. New York,
NY: St. Martin's Griffin; First edition (July 22, 2014)

Taylor, Beth, and Karen Shaw Becker, *Dr. Becker's Real Food for Healthy Dogs and Cats*. USA: Natural Pet Productions, December 1st 2009

MISCELLANEOUS WEBSITES AND BLOGS

Good Dog Service Canines (www.gooddogservicecanines.org)

Hemangiosarcoma Diet & Supplement Protocols for Dogs—A Holistic Approach (www.facebook.com/groups/422464568087083)

Keep the Tail Waggin' (www.keepthetailwagging.com)

KetoPet Sanctuary (www.ketopetsanctuary.com)

Kristen Kidd Photography (www.kristenkiddphotography.com)

Living with Dogs with Disabilities (www.facebook.com/groups/LivingwithDogswithDisabilities)

National Disaster Search Dog Foundation (www.searchdogfoundation.org)

Planet Paws (www.planetpaws.ca)

Repawsitory (www.repawsitory.com)

The Natural Canine Kitchen (www.thenaturalcaninekitchen.com)

Truth about Pet Food (www.truthaboutpetfood.com)

Upright Canine Brigade—Megaesophagus Awareness and Support (www.facebook.com/groups/uprightcaninebrigade)

Waggin' Train—Audrey Arturo certified dog trainer (www.waggintrain-nj.com)

ACKNOWLEDGMENTS

First and foremost, I would like to thank my wife, Michele Allen. Without her love and dedication to the homeless hospice dogs that deserve to live out their lives with compassion, there would be no Monkey's House. Many of the heartfelt stories she told over the years are included in this book. Thank you for creating so many great memories with me and our furry family over the years. It is a pleasure to share their final journeys with the world.

There are many others I want to thank in making *Where Dogs Go to Live: Inspiring Stories of Hospice Dogs Living in the Moment* a special tribute to not only the dogs of Monkey's House but also hospice dogs everywhere, including:

Larissa Wohl, for taking part in this project with your wonderful "Foreword," but equally so for your dedication to homeless pets everywhere. You truly do fit the role of Pet Rescue Expert. We enjoy watching you daily on the Hallmark Channel bringing comfort and love to those dogs looking for a comfy bed and a warm home.

Tracey Mauro, for your heartfelt piece, "For the Love of Smalls," and your support throughout the entire process. From the first day you walked into Monkey's House, you gave all your love to the dogs, but those smalls really grabbed your heart and soul.

Betty Woody, for your beautiful eulogy of Much Loved Bob, that little beagle that adorns the cover. When I first read it back in 2017, the day MLBob made his way to the Rainbow Bridge, I knew I would be sharing it with a much larger audience someday. It's our Monkey's House family, folks like you and thousands of others who give us the strength to continue on.

Laura Sylvester, Executive Director of Good Dog Service Canines, for your beautiful story on the magical connection between your son Elliot and his service dog Orbit. Your organization is doing wonders helping children and families live better lives with the help of autism service dogs.

Denise Sanders, Director of Communications at the Search Dog Foundation, for adding to our story on Pete's one last save. We love that your organization turns shelter dogs into search and rescue dogs, giving both the dog and human a second chance at life.

Karen Packard, for your love of all the pups, but especially your royal treatment of Princess Granny and your lovely testimony truly befitting the royalty she was.

Madalyn Stone, who helped turn this collection of furry adventures into a future best seller with her magical editing skills. I can tell a good story, and the dogs provide great material, but Madalyn turned it into a finished book. Madalyn told me she often takes walks in the park in New York City and notices many dogs, many senior pups, too. After her first pass of the manuscript, she told me something changed on her walks. Madalyn said she now has a different outlook on the senior dogs, no longer feeling sorrow as they struggle with their aging bodies, but seeing the joy in their faces living life to their fullest ability with the love and support of their adoring pet parents.

Christy Collins of Constellation Book Services for being so under-standing about all my iterations for the book cover and interior layout. You helped me craft a simple, clean, powerful cover and laid out the book wonderfully, which I know incorporating over fifty photos didn't make it easy.

Kristen Kidd of Kristen Kidd Photography for being so gracious in stepping in and preparing my pictures to be print-ready. I want to especially thank you for the photo shoot with Michele and me as many of those pictures made their way into the book.

A big thank you for all those who were willing to take the time to provide a genuine endorsement. I had an amazing response from world-class leaders in their areas of expertise who wanted to provide a few kind words about a book on hospice dogs: veterinarians Dr. Karen Shaw Becker, Dr. Peter Dobias, Dr. M Noelle Knight, and Dr. Judy Morgan; authors Jack Canfield, Laura T. Coffey, and David Rosenfelt; members of fellow rescue organizations, Sherri Franklin, Judith and Lee Piper; animal advocate Rodney Habib; lead singer of The Oak Ridge Boys, Joseph S Bonsall.

Thank you to those who read my manuscript and provided insightful feedback, allowing me to fine-tune my stories to ensure they resonated with the reader: Robert Caivano, Terresa Flannery, Marcia Horner, Michele Janesko, Vicki Masterson, Susan Power-Miller, Dr. Judy Morgan, and Susan Russell.

Thanks to my various coaches who have played a part in making this book possible: Geoffrey Berwind, Debra Englander, Raia King, Cristina Smith, and Steve Harrison.

Thank you, Patricia Allsebrook, for your assistance on managing many aspects of the book's marketing and promotion to get our story told and our mission "out there." We hope this book will influence more folks to rescue a senior dog with medical issues.

Thank you to my "Pawsome Launch Team" that helped spread the word about a book on hospice dogs living in the moment in a place called Monkey's House.

To all the aunts and uncles of Monkey's House, you're all a huge part of the dogs' lives and their adventures highlighted in this book. I'm sure you will all laugh and cry, but most of all, your hearts will be at peace reminiscing about those special moments shared together with your lovable furry friends.

To my colleagues, Thelma Slomeana, who loved reading my early drafts and always gave me rave reviews telling me I was a great writer, and Caitlin Bluem, who would then bring me back to earth with plenty of constructive feedback. You inspired me to continue on.

Finally, with all my heart and deepest gratitude, I thank the dogs that came into our lives. They gave us all so many great moments and gave me the inspiration to write this book. But more importantly, they changed our lives and opened up a new world of compassion and love.

YOUR STORY

Do you have a heartwarming story about your dog's final chapter that you would love to share? What were the challenges you faced together and how did you deal with them to create a "new normal" for your fur baby? And in your journey to make sure your dog "lived" its life to the fullest, did you find purpose in yours? How did you enjoy this precious time you had together?

We're looking for pet parents to tell us their stories that we might include in a future book. Parents whose best friend may be at the Rainbow Bridge or those who are still cherishing time with their pup. How did you make those "special moments" count? Like Tequilla loving the Jersey Shore, was there an oasis that you both enjoyed? Maybe your pup had mobility issues like Dozer or Ariel; how did you make sure its disability did not mean an inability to enjoy life?

The story of the special bond we have with our dogs that becomes even stronger in their final days needs to be told. We would love to hear your special story.

If you would like to share and inspire others, please visit:

www.monkeyshouse.org

"Special moments can be as simple as
the warmth of togetherness."

–Michele Allen with Tequilla

Photo courtesy of Kristen Kidd Photography

ABOUT THE AUTHOR

JEFF ALLEN is the cofounder of Monkey's House a Dog Hospice & Sanctuary, est. 2015. He leads a duel life helping people and dogs alike as a manager in Human Resources at a pharmaceutical company and by running Monkey's House (www.monkeyshouse.org) with his wife, Michele Allen, member of the International Association for Animal Hospice and Palliative Care, and a *2017 CNN Hero recipient*. Their sanctuary has been recognized for its outstanding work saving and caring for hospice dogs and was awarded Rescue of the Year in 2017 by World Dog Expo. Living a life among twenty-five hospice dogs has given Jeff the experience and hands-on knowledge you can't find in a book. He and Michele live in Southern New Jersey with their pack of furry kids.

Photo courtesy of Kristen Kidd Photography

Jeff and Michele with a few of the Monkey's House's pups.
Photo courtesy of Kristen Kidd Photography